No.19

No.23

No.21

No.25

No.22

No.26

Examples of the covers of the Large Notebooks

ISBN 978-1-904446-27-9

British Library Cataloguing in Publication Data
Pamela Cooksey 2010
Joseph Wood 1750-1821   A Yorkshire Quaker

To Shirley
Trust you will enjoy
Joseph
Pam

Printed and published by
Quacks Books
Petergate
York YO1 7HU

JOSEPH WOOD
1750-1821
A YORKSHIRE QUAKER

AN INTRODUCTION TO HIS LIFE, MINISTRY AND WRITINGS

Pamela Cooksey

The Large Notebooks of Joseph Wood

CONTENTS

		Page
Preface		i
Acknowledgements		ii
Introduction		1
Joseph Wood	Life	8
	Faith	37
	Ministry	51
	Writings	65
	Memoranda	66
	Accounts of Journeys	71
	Accounts of Meetings	75
	Letters	87
	Selected Quaker Writings	103
A personal conclusion		108
Appendices		109

ye Contented Quakers

Illustration from the cover of Small Notebook 27

PREFACE

I first encountered Joseph Wood when researching the history of our house, The Ridings, Thongsbridge, which is situated near Wooldale in the Holme Valley, West Yorkshire.

It was whilst reading Plain Country Friends, The Quakers of Wooldale, High Flatts and Midhope by David Bower and John Knight that I discovered in November 1778 Joseph had visited the then occupant, Joshua Broadhead, and his family. The details of this visit are to be found in one of the many Notebooks which Joseph wrote throughout his adult life. I was interested in finding out whether that occasion had been his only visit or if there were records of more and also for what purposes these had been made. A conversation with David Bower led to a meeting with James Wood of Dundee, the Custodian of the Collection of the Joseph Wood Papers.

Entry of Joseph Wood's visit to Ridings in November 1778
(Small Notebook 12 p10)

It was clear from discussions with David that Joseph's writings were exceptional. As a hitherto virtually unknown resource, they would provide a most valuable contribution to Quaker studies if they could be made available. The possibility of my making a transcription of the Notebooks was then considered, and I agreed to seek James Wood's consent for the project. This was readily given, and in January

2005 the work began, the extent of the task only then being fully recognised, for there are forty Large Notebooks and sixty-three Small Notebooks. The full transcript of the Notebooks will soon be available in the Library at Friends House in London and other centres for Quaker studies. (See Appendix 2)

As the transcribing progressed the question of how best to approach the publishing of this material arose. Following discussions with Beverley Kemp, Archivist at Friends House, London and William K. Sessions of York, it was agreed that an appropriate way forward would be for me to write an introductory book on the life, ministry and writings of Joseph Wood, prior to the publication of the transcript of the full text of all the Notebooks.

ACKNOWLEDGEMENTS

I would like to thank James Wood for allowing Joseph's writings to be made available, for agreeing to my transcribing the Notebooks and his decision to gift the Joseph Wood Collection of Papers to the Library of the Society of Friends. In relation to this book I have appreciated his interest in the project, his making the Collection of Miscellaneous Papers available to me and his help with the details of the family tree.

I am deeply grateful to David Bower for his interest in and commitment to the publishing of Joseph's writings. I am particularly indebted to him for his assistance in the determining of matters relating to Joseph's faith and for the many hours he has spent with me proof-reading the transcripts of the Notebooks.

I have appreciated the assistance of the Archivists at Friends House in London. Heather Rowland and the present Archivist, Beverley Kemp, have been generous in the time they have spent with me discussing matters relating to the transcripts, and I thank them for their interest and valuable advice.

Ben Pink Dandelion, Honorary Professor of Quaker Studies,

University of Birmingham and Programmes Leader, Centre for Postgraduate Studies, Woodbrooke Quaker Study Centre and Birmingham University has provided support and encouragement which have been greatly appreciated as has his confirmation of the significance of Joseph's writings for present and future Quaker Studies.

I was delighted when Edward Milligan, retired Librarian at Friends House, London, agreed to read a draft copy of the book and I thank him for his most valuable comments.

I would like to thank Caroline Walton (a descendant of Joseph from the family of his nephew, Robert) for her interest in the writing of this book and for making her family papers and the photographs of Joseph and the chair from the family home available to me.

David Butler has allowed me to include drawings of Meeting Houses from his book The Quaker Meeting Houses of Britain. David Cockman has prepared the cover and the illustrations. These have all greatly enhanced the text and I am very grateful to both of them.

Illustrative material relating to Records of Quaker Meetings is reproduced with the permission of Central Yorkshire Area Meeting (formerly Pontefract Monthly Meeting) and the silhouette of Esther Tuke and drawing of Thomas Shillitoe are from the Picture Collection of the Library at Friends House, London.

I would like to thank Anthony Wells-Cole, formerly the Senior Curator of Temple Newsome Leeds, for establishing the importance of the contemporary paper covers of the Notebooks and Barbara Walker for her enthusiastic investigations into contemporary papers and book making.

I am most grateful to Joan Moody for the hours she spent with me proof-reading many of the Large Notebooks and similarly to Wendy Colley for undertaking the formidable task of compiling the indexes for both the Large and Small Notebooks.

My thanks also are given to Peter Daniels, Margaret Eve, Pauline Rawlinson, and Kevin Chandler who during the writing of the book have offered me their constructive and useful comments.

I am especially grateful to Clive Watkins for his most helpful editorial assistance.

The publication of this book has received financial support from the following Quaker Trusts; Priestroyds Trust, Barnsley Adult School Trust Fund, C.B. & H.H. Taylor 1984 Trust, and the Westcroft Trust. I am greatly indebted to those concerned for their support. The proceeds from sales will be donated to High Flatts Meeting.

The transcribing of Joseph's writings has been a long, immensely time consuming but hugely enjoyable undertaking. Without the continued patient support of my husband, Graham, the project would not have been completed nor this introductory book written, for this I am deeply grateful.

INTRODUCTION
The Collection of Joseph Wood Papers:
Large and Small Notebooks

At the present time little is generally known of Joseph Wood (1750-1821) of High Flatts near Penistone in Yorkshire, his life and ministry. He was, however, a prolific writer, and many of his extensive and detailed texts, written continuously from 1767 to 1821, have survived. Carefully kept by Joseph and then by subsequent members of the family, his Notebooks and a selection of miscellaneous letters and articles have been preserved as part of a private collection. This book, based on their contents, offers the reader an introduction to this remarkable man and his quite extraordinary writings.

The unedited Notebooks include memoranda, accounts of journeys and Meetings, letters and selected Quaker writings. Effectively evoking the spirit of the times in which he lived these present to the reader an intimate and revealing portrayal of his life as a Quaker and as a member of his local community.

At sometime in the past the Notebooks have been renumbered. The Large Notebooks were placed in chronological order irrespective of the content. Seven miscellaneous books (two not written by Joseph) were added to the Small Notebooks. The original numbers, written in italics, are still visible on many of the covers. It is, however, the later numbering which is used in the printed transcription of the Notebooks and for the references in this book.

The transcription has been made as faithfully as was possible to the original text. Spelling, punctuation and the use of capital letters are unaltered, remaining as used by Joseph Wood and the writers of the material he copied. Written in a firm, consistent hand the text well demonstrates the ambiguities of the grammar of written English in the late 1700s and early 1800s. The variable spelling of words, occurring frequently in the same passage, and the inconsistent use of punctuation, capital letters and irregular use of tenses are to be found throughout. Much of Joseph's language was that which had common usage amongst Quakers. In describing the exact nature of what he was recording or writing about he used specific words and particular phrases, the precise nature of which would have been readily comprehended at the time.

Extracts from the Notebooks, have been introduced within the text, to illustrate aspects of Joseph's religious beliefs and his interpretation of these in his own life and in the lives of the people he knew. To provide a sense of Joseph's style, such extracts, presented in *italics*, are as originally written. My experience has been that if Joseph's words are read aloud, they come alive and the impact of the content is more readily appreciated. References to the quotations are given in brackets with a page number, i.e. S.N. Small Notebook, L.N. Large Notebook.

All other quotations are taken from letters Joseph received, manuscript sources and printed books. These appear in the text within inverted commas and not in italics. The details of these quotations are given in Appendix 1.

It is hoped that knowledge of Joseph and his writings will arouse interest in the full transcript of the Notebooks. When published this will provide those undertaking Quaker studies with highly significant new material relating to Quakerism in the Quietist period.

The covers of all the Large Notebooks and forty-three of the Small Notebooks are made from variously coloured and patterned decorative papers and wallpapers. Of the Small Notebooks, eight covers have pen drawn illustrations depicting scenes, people or children's games.   Twelve are covered with plain brown paper.

The nature of the decorative papers and the wallpapers and the way in which they came to be used is a matter of ongoing investigation. The three categories into which the papers fall are paste and marble papers, contemporary prints and decorative papers. It is thought that many of these were originally printed as wallpapers. It is known that paste papers (S.N.6) and marbled papers (L.N.4), were both commonly used as soft backed book covers at the time when Joseph was writing. It would appear however, that many of the other papers were not originally intended as book covers. A number of the contemporary prints are not centred on the covers (S.N.27) and other examples show that the pattern is of too large a scale to have been designed specifically as book covers. (S.N.61)   During the period when the Notebooks were covered, wallpapers were printed on rolls of paper made from hand-made sheets glued together.   The covers of many of the Notebooks show evidence of these joins (S.N.33). It seems therefore that the majority of the covers were made from wallpaper remnants and as such provide a new and significant archive spanning fifty five years.

Family historians will find the transcripts a useful resource, for the Notebooks contain hundreds of names of those belonging to Quaker families, the neighbourhoods where they lived and the Meetings they attended. A compilation of these, Quaker Families noted in the writings of Joseph Wood (1750-1821) A Yorkshire Quaker, will be available in the spring of 2011. (See Appendix 3). The detailed information regarding issues such as employment, settlements, customs and traditions, highways, routes travelled and coaching inns will be of interest to social historians.

Miscellaneous Papers

Six hundred and forty seven hand written letters received by Joseph form the major part of this collection. Catalogued according to the writer these are awaiting transcription. There is also Quaker printed material consisting of copies of London Yearly Meeting Epistles and Queries, religious tracts and Testimonies.

Contemporary Historical Context

Joseph lived through a period of turbulence and historical significance. The nation was facing unrest, discontent and dissension at home and war dominated abroad. Nowhere in his writings did Joseph refer directly to these realities but that did not mean he was ignorant of them or of their implications. In his Notebooks there are a number of articles, letters and records which indicate that he was fully aware of them and the consequences for those involved.

The major international conflicts were the American War of Independence (1775 to 1783), the French Revolution (1789-1799), and the war between England and France which lasted from 1793 until the Treaty of Amiens in 1815, with an intermission in 1802 to 1803. The Peninsular War broke out in 1808 in which Britain, Spain and Portugal fought Napoleon's forces, hostilities with the French not ceasing until the defeat of Napoleon by the Prussians and the English in 1815.

At home the country was experiencing a time of radical social and political upheaval. Far-reaching changes were taking place within society arising from industrialisation and urbanisation. Where people lived and how they earned a living, were fundamentally changing. Many workers and their families experienced the unrelenting difficulties associated with dislocation and the challenges that confronted those with redundant labour skills and working practices. Grievances were intensified by taxation, land enclosures, and the introduction of the Corn Laws.

There was a growing fear of the new political, social and philosophical ideas, particularly those coming across the Channel. The Government deeply fearful of these finding widespread support amongst those demanding political and social reform, was very ready to support the use of the militia to suppress any signs of agitation and encouraged swift and severe penalties for those involved in such activities.

The religious freedom created by the Act of Toleration passed in 1689, allowed people to gather for worship according to personal belief and to own buildings for this purpose. For Quakers the years of the late seventeenth and early eighteenth centuries are now recognised as the Quietist period of Quakerism. This was a time when the faithful were committed to preserving the spiritual truths that lay within the testimonies of the early Quakers and to maintaining their values. They were also deeply concerned to secure for themselves an identity as the Lord's *"peculiar people"* who, as such, lived separated from the world of men. The organisation required by a rapidly developing movement was created and consolidated with the establishment of Monthly, Quarterly, Yearly Meetings and Meetings for Ministers and Elders, on a local, regional and national basis. The distinguishing features of faith and behaviour were strengthened by the creation of the Book of Discipline and the annual publication of Queries to be answered by all members. In these, emphasis was placed on the unity of members, fair dealings with others, the rearing of children, the keeping of the Testimonies against the paying of Tythes or the Church Rate and the Militia and the maintaining of plainness in apparel, speech and behaviour.

Worship during the Quietist years was characterised by "vigorous vocal ministry, including lengthy sermons expounding the Truth as laid out in the scriptures and opened to Friends by the Holy Spirit" (Samuel). An equally valued facet was the "*silence*" in which those gathered together shared a collective "*waiting upon the Almighty*." The seeking of "*an inward silence*" was the duty of each individual. "This inward withdrawal made possible a tendering of the spirit in which the imagination could be set free to sense the human condition of another, while offering a man release from anxiety about his own" (Loukes). Reason and intellectual thought were to have no place in spiritual matters and religious faith; academic learning was to be shunned as being an activity of men. True knowledge was to be gained solely from the Almighty, this being revealed in the secret of a believer's soul.

In many of those who laboured in the Lord's name, the robust confidence with which the early Quakers had embraced their evangelistic endeavours was replaced by a subdued caution. Striving to determine what the Lord required of them they believed that the impetus for action and the manner of its undertaking were made known to them in "*a state of inward waiting*". It was then when all personal wishes and intentions were set aside that they became receptive to "*the promptings of the Lord.*"

Joseph lived during these Quietist years and the major interest in his Notebooks lies in his personal perspective on, and detailed insight into, the religious principles and practices of those belonging to "*a People called the Quakers,*" during this period. The material recorded deals principally with the religious beliefs and convictions of ordinary people who were Quakers and the place of religious faith in an individual's daily living and behaviour. It also reveals much about the nature of the corporate life of those who belonged to the Society of Friends.

Equally significant is the extent to which his writings reveal the nature of Joseph himself and the character and abilities that made him such an influential person and powerful preacher.

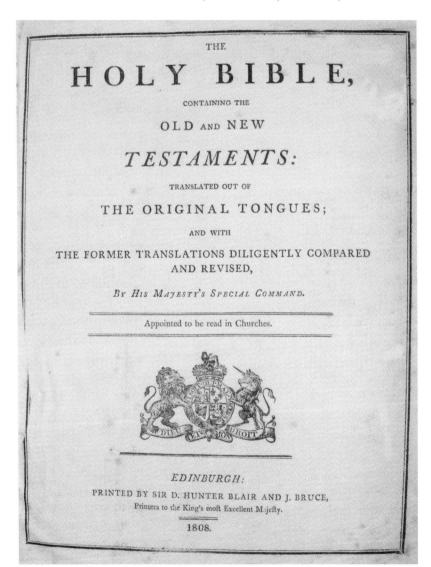

A contemporary Bible 1808

THE LIFE OF JOSEPH WOOD

Joseph Wood, the eldest of the seven children of Samuel Wood (1719-1791) and his wife Susannah (nee Walker 1722-1793), was born on the 15th February 1750 at Newhouse, near High Flatts, a small hamlet situated four miles from Penistone. (See Map, Appendix 4)

Several generations of his forbears had lived in the surrounding district, his great-great-grandfather, Abraham Wood (b1624) a wool comber lived in Shelley; his son John (b1647), with his wife Jane (nee Haigh), tenanted a farm, Wetherwood Hall, at Denby; their son, Abraham (1673-1747), after his marriage in 1703, to Rebecca Green, daughter of Joshua Green of Newhouse made his home with his father-in-law. On Joshua's death in 1710, he took over the tenancy of the farm on a twenty-one year lease at an annual rent of fourteen pounds and sixpence. Combining his work as a farmer and a clothier, Abraham, a hardworking and thrifty Quaker, was able to secure a financial standing that allowed him on occasions to advance a loan when requested. On Abraham's death in 1747, it was his only surviving son, Samuel (1719 -1791), who became tenant.

The small Jacobean farmhouse then became home to Samuel, his wife Susannah and their children - Joseph (1750-1821), Samuel (1752-1842), Sarah (1754-1757), Mary (1756-1776), Abraham (1759-1774), Susannah (1762-1787) and Rebecca (1766-1790).

Having formally served his apprenticeship as a clothier with his father, Samuel, like his father before him, continued to divide his energies between farming and the work of a clothier. Producing two pieces of hand-woven cloth a week (this being considered quite unusual at the time) he proved himself to be a successful clothier who, in his turn, apprenticed his sons, Joseph and Samuel, to the trade.

Lying within the estate belonging to the Bosville family of Gunthwaite Hall, the fifty acres of land at Newhouse supported a farm that was both productive and profitable. It was bounded to the east by woods through which streams ran to Dikeside (Denby Dale) before joining the river Dearne, and to the west by a long stretch of moorland, a sheep-walk known locally as *"Vast and Wide."* It also consisted of old enclosures, where a variety of arable crops were grown. In recognition of Samuel's industrious and careful use and maintenance of the farm, his landlord, William Bosville, offered him a lease on the farm for as long as he wanted at a rent of twenty pounds per year.

It would appear that Joseph's grandfather, Abraham Wood, was the first member of the Wood family to become a Quaker. He married Rebecca, the daughter of a Quaker, Joshua Green, who, prior to moving to Newhouse, had lived at Langsett.

In 1814 Joseph visited this house *"to look over the house from whence my Great Grandfather Joshua Green came from to Newhouse. I was much pleased with seeing the habitation of my ancestors where a meeting was held in the early time of friends"* (L.N.34 p8*)*. The circumstances of Abraham's convincement and acceptance as a member of the Religious Society of Friends have not yet been established, but it is highly likely that this would have been prior to his marriage. When writing to his cousin, Benjamin Stead, Joseph made a reference to the fact: *"We are very nearly allied to each other, by the ties of relationship, descended from one pious stock, our Grandfather and Grandmother are as I have heard being such as truly feared the Lord, and were concerned to serve him faithfully in their day; He having after his convincement and reception of the blessed truth, a Publick testimony given to bear thereunto which was acceptable to friends"* (L.B.12 p2).

It was, however, his son, Samuel, who was openly denounced and imprisoned for three months for refusing to pay the Church Tythe.

1746   Abraham Wood (Grandfather)

1771   Samuel Wood (Father)

1792   Joseph Wood

These entries taken from the Book of Sufferings for Pontefract Monthly Meeting show a continuing upholding of the Testimony against the Paying of the Church Tythe, Rate or Modus by members of the Wood family.

True to his acceptance of Quaker belief Samuel remained a diligent life-long member of High Flatts Meeting.

The foremost influence on Joseph, as a child, was thus the belief of his parents in spiritual truth as professed by the Quakers. The nurture and upbringing of their children and all aspects of family life were determined by the tenets of their faith and their membership of a Quaker community.

Meeting House at High Flatts   Seats for Elders and Ministers

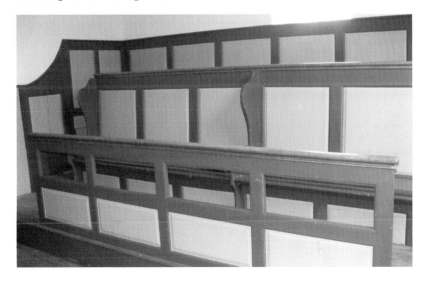

Letter to Joseph from his parents at the time of the birth of his brother Abraham.

Newhouse 16th day of 11 month 1759.
Joseph Wood these few lines coums to let the know that who ar in good helth all but thy mother for she was brought in to bed of a son on ferst day last and who hops is likely to sufer pretty Wel and I call my son Abraham Wood and thy brother Samuel went to John Earnshaws last fourt Day and Liks verey well for the time and thy Sister Mary is well and I Disier the to be a good Lad and to send hus a Lin or too when anoppertunety sarss how thy Uncle and thy Aunt Dus and thy self a Long with them so … …..   With our Dear Lof to the
from thy Loving Father and Mother   (J.W. Misc. Papers)

Joseph clearly valued the close relationships he shared with his parents, brothers and sisters. His ready insistence that *"it might be of singular service to many families were they more generally in the practice of collecting together on First day evenings and one after another reading a chapter in the Scriptures; the rest sitting quietly to hear, and after this was done closing with a time of solemn silence, in which if Parents are deep and weighty in their spirits, I doubt not but they would at times be favoured to drop some suitable counsel and Advice to their Children and servants, which would prove a blessing unto them"* (L.N.15 p11) may well reflect not only his approval of the practice and his valuing of the nature of such *"opportunities"* but also his experiences of his childhood and family life at Newhouse.

From Joseph's writings there is no reason to think that his father was anything other than supportive of his son's decision to commit his life to the service of the Lord. Samuel appears to have accepted the implications of his son's withdrawal from the weaving work of their business as clothiers. The frequent and often lengthy absences that Joseph had from home were made with his consent. He sometimes met Joseph as he was returning from one of his journeys and together they would then go to a local Meeting. On the death of his father, in 1791, Joseph inherited the tenancy of Newhouse. Of his father Joseph recorded: *"He was an affectionate Husband, a tender Parent, a kind Relation, a good Master, a peaceful neighbour a sincere and honest Man, just in all his dealings, and concern'd to fulfil his engagements with punctuality, endeavouring to do unto all men as he would have them do unto him, and was generally beloved by all who knew him"* (L.N.5 p22).

The illness and death of his mother two years later troubled him greatly. He had had for some time, *"a concern"* on his mind to attend Knaresborough Monthly Meeting, and as the day of his departure drew near, he noted: *"my Spirit was under great heaviness upon the account of my Mothers indisposition believing her not to be far from her conclusion which brought me into a very great strait, when I turned inward I seem'd not easy to stay, but when the reasoning part got uppermost the thoughts if I should never see her any more alive made me exceeding sad and ready to desire to be excused until the language of Christ was brought before me, that if we did not leave all for his sake and the Gospels we were not worthy of him and she being I believe in some measure sensible of my concern not only freely gave me up but encouraged me to set forward which I did, after taking a very solemn Farewell of her."* At Otley, on the third day of his journey to attend the Monthly Meeting, he recalled: *"I was walking down the street towards it, I was led to remember my Mother whom I had left ill behind and was so affected therewith as scarcely to refrain from weeping."* After her death he wrote: *"She was a tender Mother, a good mistress, a kind neighbour, charitable to the poor, administering to their relief according to her ability and hath left a good report behind her; she had been afflicted with a rheumatic complaint for many years, which increasing upon her wholly confin'd her to her Bed the last 22 weeks of her time, her afflictions were very great yet she was enabled to bear them with a good degree of patience expressing her full assurance of eternal felicity hereafter"* (S.N.22 p5).

Joseph was seven when his sister Sarah died. Only brief reference was made to his other sisters, Susannah and Rebecca, in his memoranda and that relating to their sickness and death. When visiting or travelling through Sheffield he often slept or dined at the home of Susannah and her husband, Daniel Doncaster. His great distress on receiving the news of Susannah's death is clearly evident from his account of her burial at which he noted that he *"was much effected with seeing the remains of my poor sister"* (S.N.17 p16).

Two letters have survived written during the time his youngest brother, Abraham, was apprenticed to Joseph Awmack, Grocer, of York. Joseph wrote to him: *"let me desire thee in much Affection to be a good Boy and in the first Place seek the kingdom of Heaven and the Righteousness thereof and then I make no doubt but all things needful will be added thou will then be beloved of God and good Men. Be obedient to thy Master and Mistress and diligent in their Business not serving them with Eye service but with singleness of Heart Keep good Company and spend Part of thy Leisure Hours in reading especially the Holy Scriptures and if thou can get a Copy of John Woolmans Testimony I desire thee to be so kind as to Write it down and send it to me as soon as thou can for I and many others would be glad to see it"* (J.W. Misc. Papers).

Tragically Abraham died later in the year, after having, it is thought, committed suicide, (John Wood). A strange occurrence, for from a letter written to Joseph only a few weeks before his death, it appears nothing seems to have been amiss as he recounted his pleasure at seeing family members at a Meeting in York and of being "at Skipton helping gather the harvest for my Master's brother" (J.W. Misc. Papers).

The exact nature of Joseph's relationship with his surviving brother Samuel is unclear. The many entries in his memoranda show that they were frequently in each others company for Joseph called, on many occasions, at his house when returning from Meetings. Nowhere did he make any reference to the difficult circumstances that resulted from the fact that Samuel preferred drinking and hunting to maintaining a profitable business or to the distress that this situation caused all the family. Joseph must have been deeply troubled by his brother's behaviour which will have assuredly incurred his severest condemnation. It is clear from the contents of some of his letters he recorded in his Notebooks that those who spent time frequenting ale houses or who were engaged in vain sports (of which hunting was one) received letters from him in which he censured their conduct and urged them to amend their ways.

Joseph enjoyed a warm relationship with the many relatives within his extended family. Numbered amongst the accounts

Letter written by Joseph to his brother, Abraham, when he began his apprenticeship in York

(J.W. Misc. Papers)

of his social and religious visits and journeys to Meetings are those to family members. On many occasions, when returning to Newhouse after attending a local or more distant Meeting, he would call in on the families of his uncles, cousins, and his nephew, Robert.

Attending the small boarding school run by Joseph Shaw in the neighbouring Quaker hamlet of High Flatts Joseph had received a basic education. Fifty boys were taught in the Meeting House and boarded at the homes of Edward Dickinson and Joseph Shaw. Surviving letters and Joseph's accounts of having lodged whilst travelling with one-time fellow pupils reveal that friendships established during this time continued for many years.

Recalling his youth, Joseph confessed to John Walker of Batty Mill near Thurlstone, without giving details, of *"having trod the slippery paths of youth myself and been acquainted with the temptations and snares of the unwearied enemy and the propensities of mans nature to evil"* (L.N.10 p4). During those years a growing awareness of the folly of his behaviour and a deepening realisation of the error of his way of living caused him to suffer great distress. The Testimony to his life produced by the members of Pontefract Monthly Meeting stated: "In his youth he gave way to some of the vanities incident to that period of Life for when approaching manhood, he was happily brought under the sustaining power of Truth and often humbled in great contrition of soul before the Lord. During this season of deep inward exercise, he has since related that once in his extremity being out in the Fields in the Night he exclaimed Lord what shall I do or wither shall I go? The answer in the secret of his own Heart was as intelligible as if spoken in his outward Ear. Whither wilt thou go have not I the words of Eternal life? Soon after he attended a neighbouring Meeting when a Ministering Friend who was a stranger stood up in testimony with the very words which he had received as an answer to his inquiry and who afterwards enlarged upon the subject in a manner suited to his state of Mind. This circumstance yielded him both consolation and great encouragement".

At the age of seventeen he took the decision to submit himself to the will of the Lord and to devote his life to serving Him. It was then that he began to travel throughout Yorkshire, Derbyshire, Westmorland, Lancashire, Nottinghamshire, Cheshire, Durham and Wales attending Quaker Meetings.

Writing of William Earnshaw of Wooldale, an Elder, who had greatly influenced him in his youth, Joseph wrote: *"a sense of thy Fatherly and Parental regard, many times manifested to me when in the infancy in religious experience demands my grateful acknowledgement thereof to thee"* (L.N.12 p11).

His account to Elizabeth Dickinson of the profound influence other Elders of High Flatts Meeting had had on him stated: *"those solid grave ancient friends who were weightily exercised in spirit for the arising of Life, whose countenances being enlivened by the pure Truth were a blessing to the meeting; I well remember the effect it had upon my mind, when I have seen the tears trickle down their venerable cheeks"* (L.N.33 p16).

The highly esteemed Quaker Minister, Esther Tuke, whose ability to inspire the young was well known, recognised Joseph as a young man with strong spiritual convictions. Samuel Tuke, wrote of his grandmother: "She was lively and spirited, and had a natural facetiousness and at the same time a dignity of mien which gave her an invincible influence over the minds of young persons" (Tylor). Esther took a personal interest in Joseph's progress in the life he had chosen encouraging him as he responded to the leadings of the Lord. To this end she wrote to him: "in supporting and encouraging thee to perseverance on the path thy feet are happily turned into, as much depends upon it, not only on thine own account but others to whom thou hast and I believe will still be exceeding helpful, thy readiness to promote the Cause and at every opportunity likely to forward the work, an offering acceptable in the sight of God" and "as thou seeks and follows the dictates of true wisdom thy labours will be blessed" (L.N.2 p1).

Esther Tuke 1727-1794

She concerned herself with the deepening of his faith through conversations when they met at Meetings or when Joseph visited her home in York and by letter writing. Joseph recorded that in 1777, when returning from a Meeting at Castleton in Derbyshire, whilst staying in Sheffield he attended *"the Old Meetinghouse"*. Esther was also there with several other eminent visitors and on seeing him she said that *"I might have the liberty to sit with them of which I was pleased"* (S.N.10 p11).

Anxious that he should also acquire the practical knowledge and skills that would be required of him in his service to the Lord she asked him to assist with making the arrangements for some of the public meetings she held. This offered Joseph first hand experience of working with strangers, of having to find and hire a suitable room, provide appropriate seating, which in some cases involved the constructing of a temporary gallery, publicising the event and securing overnight accommodation.

In 1779 Joseph's *"gift in Ministry"* was acknowledged by the Elders and other Ministers of the Meeting at High Flatts.
(J.W. Testimony Pontefract Mo.Mg.)

To allow the time in which he could more fully enter upon the work of the Lord, whilst retaining his farming interests and involvement in the sales of the finished cloth, Joseph gave up his responsibilities for the weaving of cloth to others. He recorded little regarding his business activities, there only being references relating to *"fetching of lime"* from Pontefract for the fields, of having to make a visit to somebody *"to attend to some business"* or when in Huddersfield he would note *"called at market"* or *"met Father at the Cloth Hall."*

For Friends attendance at fairs was permissible to accomplish some transaction of business but that done Joseph's recurring advice was that a speedy departure was required so that a believer would not be ensnared by *"the vanities, follies and sins of the world"* inherent in such gatherings. When explaining this to Joseph Haigh he wrote: *"I can say from experience that when the Lord was pleased to visit me with the day spring from on high he showed me that it was my duty to avoid attendance of these places when I could do my business elsewhere"* (L.N.10 p18). It would appear that much of the buying and selling associated with his business as a clothier was undertaken with people he met at the many Quaker Meetings he visited.

Joseph was equally concerned that people should avoid joining the crowds to see spectacles and entertainments. When returning home one day from Penistone of those present when *"They was Baiting a Bear at Bridgend"* he recorded: *"I got through them without speaking a word to any; But my heart was filled with sorrowful reflections upon the too general depravity of the People in this highly favoured land"* (L.N.20 p 19).

Whilst travelling, Joseph became known to those wishing to hire a suitable apprentice or to employ an honest servant or reliable skilled worker. He met many parents who wished their children to find employment in Quaker families and Quaker owned businesses. From his personal knowledge of the members of many Meetings it would appear that his assistance was sought in finding appropriate placements for people.

Joseph's jottings on *Places and Servants wanted*   (J.W.Misc.. Papers)

Timothy Clark of Doncaster wants an Apprentice to a Grocer fee expected
Joseph Sanders of Sheffield Gardener wants an Apprentice
Wanted at Ackworth a Person to keep the Books a Matron and a Husbandman
Peter Hardy of Bridlington at Ackworth School wants a Place an Apprentice
Sarah Kookson of Knasbor' wants a Jurniman Tallow Candler
Richard Whitehead of Knasbor' Mo. Mg. wants a place Apprentice, a Shoomaker
most agreeable
John Rountree Draper and Grocer of Scarbro' wants an Apprentice, a fee expected
Joseph Firth of Toothill wants a Husbandman
John Sutcliffe of Sheffield wants an Apprentice a fee expected

Denby

Nᵒ	rentˢ Names	Closes & Names	Quantity A	R	P	Total qu.ty A	R	P
3	Jonathan Wood	Comⁿ Close	26	..	20			
90	& his Son	Mesne Field	3	2	12			
106	Joseph Wood	Grass Yard	1	3	32			
125	do	Owlers do	..	3	36			
141	do	Lemonacre	·3	3	12	36	2	..
4	Joseph Wood of	Comⁿ Close	4	..	32			
5	New House	Well Croft	..	..	32			
6		House &c	2	..	36			
7		Great West Field	3	3	16			
9		Little do	3	..	4			
10		Long do	4	2	20			
11		Long Close	3	..	..			
12		O Lands	3	1	32			
14		Little Hey	2	2	36			
15		Great do	5	3	0			
17		Ingbrow	1	..	36			
174		Ing	5	1	24			
20		Hey	1	1	20			
22		do	2	..	20			
25		do	2	3	16	46	..	36
16	Elihu Dickinson	Long Ing	4	2	12			
18	Clothier	Steep Close	1	3	0			
19		Round Field	5	3	0			
26		Pingle	4	..	..	16	..	20
						98	3	24

The entry recording Joseph Wood's tenancy of the house and land at Newhouse from the Survey of the Bosville Estate 1807

As an owner of a flock of sheep Joseph, sharing the concerns of other clothiers and neighbouring shepherds, played a leading role in the work of the local Shepherds Society. Small Notebook 18 contains the records of the meetings of members for the years 1788 to 1800. Entries dealt with the use of the monies raised to reward those who destroyed any of the roaming dogs that killed sheep and lambs, to compensate members when they suffered such a loss and to buy tobacco, pipes, ale, bread and cheese for the enjoyment of those attending the meetings.

Entry in the Records of the Shepherds Society
(S.N.18 p3)

Following the deaths of his sisters, younger brother and parents Joseph thought of his household servants, housekeeper and husbandmen as *"my family"*. It was they who looked after his personal and domestic needs and it was to them that the responsibility for the running of his house and farm fell, particularly when he was absent from home on his journeys. *"Often have I to bless the Lord for his great mercies in favouring me when stripped of my near Relations, with a family who manifest an affectionate regard for me and a prudent care in the management of my outward affairs, but above all that several of them have closed in with the Lord according to the best of their understanding"* (S.N.26 p4). This relationship was underlined in *"An Epistle of tender Love and caution to mine own family written to William Taylor, John Bottomley, Henry Marsden, Hezekiah Smith and Frances Field.*

Let others do as they may, me and my house may serve the Lord; and being now a favoured family all of whom have been visited with the day spring from on high; my spirit hath felt a travail for your preservation, growth and establishment in pure righteousness; that so we may be as a City set upon a hill, which cannot be hid; A family of Love, manifesting to others whose disciples we are, each one being preserved in that humility of mind, as to wash one anothers feet; If we are preserved in this state of mind, altho' our gifts may be different, our respective duties unto God and one unto another will be clearly manifested, strength and ability will be afforded to come up faithfully in the discharge of the same: wherefore dearly beloveds keep in the Lords holy fear and then you will delight to attend religious meetings and as much as in you liveth order your outward affairs so as not to be prevented on weekdays, which is far as is in my Power, I hope I shall endeavour to set you at liberty so to do; having no greater joy than to see you walking in the Truth, each one endeavouring to fill up your own proper places according to the measure and manifestation of the divine gift you are favoured with. Be kindly affectioned one to another with brotherly love; in honour of preferring one another; Not slothful in business; fervent in spirit; serving the Lord; rejoicing in hope; patient in tribulation; continuing instant in Prayer. I am with unfeighned love to you all, your Brother and companion in the

tribulation and fellowship of the Gospel of Christ   *Joseph Wood"*
(L.N.17A p1).

During 1795 when Henry Marsden was nearing the end of his apprenticeship Joseph wrote to him: *"I have never looked upon thee as a servant but as a Brother beloved and have been concerned to watch over thee for good"* (L.N. 8 p2).

When recording the events of his fifty-fifth birthday, he described how, after Meeting at High Flatts: *"I had ordered supper to be provided for those of mine own house and esteemed friends John Pickford and Frances his wife and my beloved scholar Joseph Grayham. At table I looked over the company and as I looked I thought they felt as near to me as if they were my own children"* (L.N.23 p19).

The wellbeing of Joseph's *"family"* was dependant on the members' respect for and compliance with the rules and the practices of the household. When Benjamin Beever, a new employee, chose not to heed these he received from his *"truly affectionate friend and Master"* a severe rebuke: *"I feel my mind engaged from an apprehension of duty; and a real desire for thy welfare, to warn thee in future to desist from absenting thyself from my house improperly, and associating thyself with such as are seeking to draw thee into vanity of any kind, which will in the end most assuredly terminate in vexation of spirit. The Apostle declares, the wages of sin is death; but the gift of God is eternal life through Christ Jesus our Lord. Now I wish thou may just consider this seriously and the awful consequence of living in sin the punishment of which is eternal death O my dear Lad, how has my mind been of late exercised on thy account, that thou might be preserved from the evils of the world. This must be by taking heed to the gift of God in thee which comes by Jesus Christ; It will teach thee to obey thy Master in all his lawful commands; and not absent thyself from his house without his knowledge, or consent will make thee to abstain from every appearance of evil. It will teach thee thy duty unto God and man; and as thou submits unto the operation thereof will Create thee anew in*

Christ Jesus unto good works" (L.N.22 p16).

Joseph never married, although surviving letters from school friends would suggest that there was a time when those who knew him expected that he would. Thomas Hawkes replying to an enquiry made by Joseph wrote from Norwich in 1768: "To answer the next part of thy kind favour respecting Nancy Dickinson, and her cousin Polly Firth, which without doubt are both polite, accomplished, and agreeable young Women and I should suppose Nancy Sister Hannah not in the least behind either of them. Think my friend Joseph Wood might tend his present or future services to one of them or if they have not chance sufficient to attract thy attention, from the objects of the like nature then doubtless another of the fair sex either have or will have" (J.W.Misc. Papers).

Thomas Cash when writing to Joseph to order "a little cloth to make me a coat and wascoat as good as thou can afford for 5 shillings a yard the same colour as that I had from the before" also wrote concerning the son of the widow with whom he had lodged at High Flatts: "I am pleased to here he was marryed, and should be so to here of Joseph Wood being agreeable marryed" (J.W. Misc. Papers). John Wood of Newhouse stated: "the sole sacred thing in the house, a china sugar basin left by the only Lady he ever loved as far as we know" (John Wood).

An understanding of his decision to remain single, and thereby denying himself the possibility of fatherhood, can be found in a letter he wrote in which he made clear his concerns regarding the conflicting requirements of marriage and family and a full commitment to ministering in the name of the Lord. It was to John Pickford that he wrote in 1802: *"Marriage is lawful to all by the laws of man; but I believe not expedient to all. It is a comfortable state to those who are rightly joined together therein, and some are rendered more useful thereby. There are others who have been useful before, that have been little use afterwards; the necessary cares and concerns of their family preventing their growth and usefulness. It is far easier to keep the mind stayed upon the Lord whilst single, saith a worthy friend in his Journal; than when weighed down with the encumbrance of a growing family, ... And therefore I believe there are such in the present day as Christ foretold which hath made themselves eunuchs for the kingdom of heaven's sake Believing they might from the situation Providence had placed them in be more useful in their day, age and generation"* (L.N.24 p19).

Letter from Mary West to Joseph Wood

(J.W. Misc.. Papers)

Mary Wests kind respects to Mr. Wood and is sorry to inform him that she has been so unfortunate yesterday as to lose her beautyfull pea hen in consequence of fighting with another hen if Mr. W. could repair the Loss by lending or letting me have one it would greatly oblidge

Cawthorne
Wednesday Morn.

Yours Sinciarly
Mary West

Joseph, as a highly regarded member of the local community, was sometimes asked to perform certain public tasks. He served as an Overseer of the Poor and, following fatal accidents or a suicide, he was sent for by the Coroner to attend the inquest. He was seen by others as a good neighbour, a person on whom one could call for assistance. On one occasion, when visiting York, he went to the Castle to see John Kennion of Cumberworth who was imprisoned there for *"a defraud"*, his Father *"having sent him money by me"* (S.N.32 p3).   The letter Mary West wrote to him suggests that she knew well his readiness to help others.

A very sociable man, who greatly enjoyed the company of friends, both Quaker and non-Quaker, Joseph took much pleasure in calling on relatives and friends with whom he then, according to the time of day, drank tea, or coffee, took refreshment, breakfasted or dined.

He found great delight in staying with Friends in their homes and having folk come to spend time with him. The hospitality enjoyed by guests at Newhouse and "the society of its genial and saintly master were intensely appreciated by a wide circle of friends" (Mills). From Joseph's descriptions of time spent with his guests this involved comfortable and edifying conversation, long walks over the moors, time spent reading and discussing Quaker articles and epistles, attending High Flatts Meetings with their host and sharing in the after supper opportunity with the family.

Among the frequent visitors were those who travelled regularly to attend county-wide Meetings some of them Joseph's converts. One such man was William Midgely of Buersill near Rochdale. The depth of the friendship he and Joseph enjoyed is evidenced in their correspondence.

Chair from Newhouse

Many letters have survived in which those who stayed at Newhouse thanked Joseph for his company and the spiritual support they had received from him. Samuel Lloyd wrote expressing his pleasure in the days they spent together: "I suppose thou has lately been engaged on thy small farm during harvest time, when I should like very much to see thee and enjoy thy cheerful and instructive company" and "I would have very much liked to be one of the party assembled around thy blazing fire, but would prefer still more to ramble with thee into the Country with a summer's sun and enjoy thy interesting company. If I should have the course of my travels get into thy neighbourhood, whether winter or summer, I intend to seek thee out and witness the peaceful dwelling wherein thou dwells, and learn from thy pleasant though humble mansion not to covert riches, but rather better things" (J.W. Misc. Papers).

Likewise, Joseph kept an open door for those who attended Meetings at High Flatts or as they travelled to other local Meetings. Providing for his Friends in this way required of his housekeeper a willing, flexible and highly organised approach to her work for on many occasions it was without prior arrangement. Once when returning from a Monthly Meeting at High Flatts, Joseph noted: *"found several friends come to my house and some others came afterwards so I was favoured with the company of seven lodgers, many friends called and breakfasted with us but had only twelve to dine"* (L.N.24 p8), on another occasion when there were: *"13 to supper and 12 lodgers, we were obliged to get Beds for 5 of them out at our neighbours houses"* (L.N.28 p22). Recording a rare occurrence he wrote: *"we had no company today which is very unusual to dine with us today"* adding rather regretfully *"nor any to tea"* (L.N.30 p7). His was indeed a well ordered household, for he regularly noted in his memoranda how: *"whilst my family were employed in the annual cleaning of the house ... to be out of the way ... I always leave home".*

Joseph numbered amongst his friends *"those of other professions".* Interestingly three such men were the local

Clergymen with whom he could not have differed more in religious belief and practice, though this in no way prevented him from valuing their company and they his. These were the Priest of Cawthorne, the Rev. John Ball, of whom Joseph wrote: *"he always appeared particularly social and free with me........ I understood expressed a partiality for my company".* (L.N.36 p14*),* the Rev. William Railton, the Priest of Cumberworth, who he described as: *"a social friendly man and a kind neighbour"* (L.N.28 p6) and the Rev. Chadwick Hepworth of Robin Hoods Bay, a former Priest of Cumberworth, who when describing his visit to see him Joseph wrote: *"he was much pleased to see me and tho' it was but half past 10 when I got there he insisted me tarrying dinner and showed much freedom and respect to me in this way"* (S.N.4 p9).

He also greatly valued the longstanding friendship he had with Timothy Sykes, a preacher with the Methodists, who lived in Shafton near Wakefield. They corresponded frequently and called at each other's homes on many occasions, Joseph when he was visiting friends in the area and Timothy when he had a preaching engagement at the Methodist chapel at Denby Dale. To arrange such a visit Timothy wrote: "I have not till yesternight got to know when I come to Dykeside I am put down for 15th Dec' at that time if it please the Lord I shall be at Dyke and to stop all night at your house I shall be glad to have a sociale interview with you I trust you and I (though in two different partys) will experience a communion of Saints I clearly see that nothing but the power of religion in the Soul will stand in any stead when I come to lay upon a Deathbed What is all profession without the heart be renewed by divine Grace my prayer is that you and I may ever be led by the spirit of God. Dear friend I am affectionately yours"   (J.W. Misc. Papers).

Joseph would have been well aware of the dilemma Quakers faced regarding political thought and action. His clearly expressed advice to others was typified in that which he offered James Taylor of Shelley Woodhouse: *"I would tenderly intreat thee to avoid all conversation respecting Politicks; as we as a People I am* sure have no business to meddle therewith; and I fully believe whoever does amongst us, will not prosper in the Truth, but a dwindling will imperceptibility come over them; until their latter end may be worse than their beginning" (L.N.8 p10). His thinking reflected well the generally held belief that "It becometh not the members of our Society to meddle much in those matters, or to be active in political disquisitions.........In respect to elections, we ought to go no farther than voting for the candidates we best approve, and declaring our preference of them without endeavouring by any other means to influence others. Israel is to dwell alone and not to be mixed with the people" (Scott).

Writing to James Willan, he put it like this: *"we as a People profess to behave ourselves as quiet and peaceable subjects, under whatsoever form of government we are placed, not following those that are given to change, nor mixing with the World in conversation upon political subjects. Believing that we are called to shew forth unto the World in Life and conversation that the blessed reign of the Messiah the Prince of peace is begun"* (L.N.33 p18).

Despite these views, at the time of the Parliamentary Election of 1807, Joseph, being a freeholder of land in Staincross valued at more than 40 shillings, exercised his right to vote. At the Canvas he offered his vote to two of the three candidates, these being Lord Milton, the son of Earl Fitzwilliam of Wentworth Woodhouse, a Whig, and William Wilberforce the Tory anti-slavery campaigner. He no doubt justified his decision to vote on the grounds that Wilberforce was a tireless advocate for the abolition of slavery. Judging by the number of articles on the subject in his Collection of Miscellaneous Papers this was a cause to which Joseph was fully committed.

In his memorandum relating to the Election held at York he noted: *"the Milton Committee sitting at Huddersfield were very earnest to get me and some others off as speedily as they could, but I being in a poor state of health, had almost entirely dropt the thought of going to York but the contest being a very sharp one, the Committee sent a Chaise to Birdsedge for me, Elihu Dickinson Clothier and William Dickinson".* On their arrival in York, Joseph and his companions, having become aware of *"some false report having been spread very prejudicial to the Interest of William Wilberforce"*, decided *"to see him before we went to the Poll".* This they managed to do *"in a room in the Castle were he fully cleared himself of those reports".* He then stated that *"having heard it from his own mouth we were better able to contradict them afterwards"* (L.N.28 p2).

His writings reveal that, on at least one occasion, Joseph's sense of justice caused him to respond to what he considered to be an unmitigated injustice. In 1801, fiercely critical of the *"mercenary Freeholder"* taking common land under the Act of Parliament for the Inclosure of Common Land he wrote: *"I have never found it to be my business to meddle much with Publick affairs, I thought I felt most easy to commit to writing a few remarks on the present mode of Inclosing Commons".* With great understanding and profound sorrow he then described the often devastating implications for *"the Man of little property"* and the poor when they were *"deprived of their just and equitable right whereby many have been assisted in the support of their families"* (L.N.17 p12).

Joseph's upbringing meant that he was a practical man with a good understanding of the lives of many of those he encountered. When visiting a family, he would sometimes find them engaged in work on their farm, in the field, cutting hay or harvesting. In his memorandum for such a day he would note that, as he recognised the importance for farming folk of finishing the task of the day, he had given them his help before spending time in religious conversation. On one occasion sheep-shearing was underway on the farm he had called at, and when he was told that one of the shearers had failed to arrive, he did the required work himself. Being aware of the dire circumstances experienced by the poor and the destitute after visiting the families of the Luddite supporters hanged at

York Castle in 1812 he noted he had *"left a little money with each family"* (S.N.51 p9).

Albeit Joseph's writings dealt almost exclusively with his faith and religious duty, within them the reader catches a glimpse of a man who enjoyed certain personal pleasures. He clearly preferred to be shaved, for numerous journeys began with a stop at *"John Pickfords of Parkhead to be shaved"*. During his visits to friends' houses or when on a journey he called at a public house, he liked to take tea, coffee or a glass of rum or brandy with water. When relaxing, he liked nothing more than to smoke his pipe. "I hope thou as usual makes thy Pipe with our Family" was the expressed wish of Mary Dickinson in a letter she wrote him in 1794 and Robert Rhodes sent him "two holders fild thy tobbaco pat a pipe some tobbaco and a muffler of my own knitting to wean round thy neck" (J.W. Misc. Papers). It would appear that he also took pleasure in taking snuff and in the containers in which this was kept "if we are to judge by the number of his boxes for he had a whole harem of them" (John Wood). Having enjoyed a rural upbringing he delighted in the countryside and the beauty of nature. He often noted the joy he felt walking across heather- or bracken covered moorland or on hearing, as he did on the day after his sixty-ninth birthday *"the notes of the Cuckow for the first time this year"* (L.N.36 p21).

For many years Joseph experienced recurring ill health. He frequently noted *"the return of my complaint"* or made reference to suffering from *"the Flux"*, *"the Lax"* or *"the Cholick"*. The recipe for a cure for piles sent him by Robert Whitaker, would suggest that this was the painful condition that he wrote of when planning to go to a public meeting in Dronfield: *"I had not the strength to get there by foot, neither could I ride on horseback on account of a complaint"* (S.N.60 p21). When planning a religious visit with Thomas Shillitoe to the public houses in Barnsley, he wrote to his friend that *"either from cold or from some other cause"* he had been *"in a poor state of health and not knowing how long I may continue in this state, (if the Lord should be pleased to raise me up again;) I thought it best to inform thee of; when you think to commence the said visit; if I am so far restored as to think it prudent, shall endeavour to attend at the time"* (L.N.33 p16).

Of his experience during a religious visit to Derbyshire in 1818, in which he had attended Meetings, visited families of Friends and held many Public Meetings, he wrote: *"though some part of the time I was very ill, and most part of it had little sleep and a very poor appetite, yet I was not thereby hindered in my Journey, and altho' the meetings were very large and the exercise therein great yet I was enabled to go through the service required without being sensible of my infirmities"* (S.N.60 p8). On numerous occasions it must have been with great determination and fortitude that he undertook his Ministry. "During the latter period of his life, feeling his bodily strength decline he was anxiously desirous that no service required of him should be omitted. His Zeal increased with his Years and he became more and more abundant in Labor for the promotion of the Christian cause, and he was frequently out travelling on Truths service" (J.W. Testimony Pontefract Mo.Mg.). In this Testimony it was also stated that on his seventieth birthday Joseph had written in a memorandum: *"may the remainder of my days be so devoted to the Lord's service as when the solemn message of death is sent, I may have nothing to do but to render up my account with joy".*

Joseph John Gurney, of Earlham Hall, Norwich, an eminent Quaker, banker, theologian and prison reformer knew Joseph well. When Joseph, accompanied by George Breary, undertook a religious visit to Friends in Lincolnshire and Norfolk he offered them hospitality at Earlham Hall. Writing in his Journal for 24 June, 1819 he noted: "Joseph Wood and his companion breakfasted with us. After breakfast I accompanied them as guide, they in their wicker cart and I on horseback..... Joseph Wood is a deep and able Minister, a thoroughly honest, innocent man". (Braithwaite).

Joseph died, at Newhouse, on 26 March 1821, having exercised his gift as a minister forty-two years. During that time "as a fine vigorous and determined specimen of Yorkshire grit and manhood" (Mills), he became a well respected and much travelled Minister, a greatly valued friend to all those who knew him, and a tireless worker in the cause of spreading Quaker Truth, the saving of souls and maintaining the faith and discipline of the convinced.

Examples of the Small Notebook covers

THE FAITH OF JOSEPH WOOD

A profound belief in spiritual truth, as professed by Quakers, was the bedrock on which Joseph's adult life was founded. This is revealed in the numerous letters he wrote as he encouraged others to consider their lives and to reflect on the state of their souls. His common themes were the nature of God and his dealings with mankind, the fallen state of man, the realities of good and evil, the responsibility given to individuals for choice between these, the inevitability of the Lord's judgement and of heaven and hell, repentance, forgiveness and salvation. Unlike some contemporary religious belief it was not a doom laden faith. Though man's knowledge of God and his purposes was incomplete, an essential part of Joseph's faith was the conviction that, in whatever the various circumstances and situations men and women found themselves in, whatever the difficulties and hardships they had to face, if they remained faithful then *"all would work for good"* of an individual's soul. Joseph's faith was one of expectant hopefulness.

Central to his faith was a belief in the existence of the all-powerful, all- knowing and ever-present Creator. His was a God who dwelt in the heart of every man and woman. The human soul was where the *"Light and Life of God"* were manifest and the Holy Spirit, the divine power of the Lord, was experienced. It was through the power of the Holy Spirit that individuals were enlightened in the things of the spirit and empowered to order their lives in accordance with *"the measure"* of understanding and ability given them by God.

It was essential for every individual *"to know what is the will of God concerning them; to live under the influence of that divine Power of Christ which can alone renew and change the mind and restore poor and lost fallen and degenerated man unto the image of Christ whose whole Life was one continued scene of humility and self-denial, directly opposite to the customs, manners, language and fashions of a world that lieth in wickedness"* (L.N.19 p9).

For Joseph an awareness of God's presence, spiritual revelation and an understanding of the Truth were essentially based on intuition and feelings. With age, he became very wary of the influences of the thinking of the Enlightenment during the early years of the 1800s, a philosophy which demanded a rational and reasoned consideration of the human condition, including the spiritual. He felt this threatened *"the truth of the Prophets"* and *"the faith of our forefathers".* He was fearful that an argued faith would replace the God-given, personal, spontaneous response. He also feared that a doctrine formed from an intellectually conceived theology would destroy the purity of the spoken ministry.

Jesus Christ, the Son of God was *"the unspeakable gift of God"* to mankind. He was *"the mediator of the new covenant of Light and Life, the true teacher of his People, the alone way to God"* (L.N.19 p7) and *"was appointed to be Judge both of the quick and the dead"* (L.N.26 p1).

A crucial aspect of Joseph's understanding of how an individual came to a deeper knowledge of the Lord was his belief in *"the revelation of the Father manifest through the Son by the eternal spirit"* (L.N.14 p7). It was through this and faithfulness to *"his requirings"* that man would be created anew. *"I am persuaded the Seed, the precious seed of the kingdom which is Christ, is sown in thy heart and that everything may be given up by thee, that may have a tendency to hinder its growth and then I doubt not but in due time thou will be favoured to experience a Birth brought forth in thee of its own divine and heavenly nature"* (L.N.27 p19).

Joseph embraced the truths manifested within the events of Christ's life, his miracles and teachings but above all his death. God *"manifest his mercy and abundant loving kindness unto all in sending his only begotten son into the world, cloathed with human nature; who after a life of sorrow and Afflictions, suffered an ignominious and painful death upon the Cross, the just for the unjust; Thus offering himself a propitiatory sacrifice for the sins of all mankind, and purchasing that precious gift for all, by which all might come to experience their sins forgiven, their iniquity is pardoned; and then not living unto themselves, but unto him who died for them; might be favoured to glorify him here on earth, and eternally so in heaven"* (L.N.15 p9).   Joseph believed that he was one for whom *"the Lords mercy doth appear through him who was wounded for mans transgression and by whose stripes the remnant of those who are saved are healed".*   Individual men and women were to *"live under the discipline of the cross of Christ by which they experience a being crucified to the world and the world to them"* (L.N.14 p4).

It was through Christ, *"who hath done so much in order to reconcile poor fallen, lost, degenerate man unto his maker"* (L.N.14 p6) that the new covenant between God and mankind was created, *"the covenant being changed, the law which was formerly outward wrote upon tables of stone is now inward, wrote in the heart"* (L.N.26 p15).   Men and women were to acknowledge with thanks *"what a favour it is to be brought under the new covenant dispensations in which none need say unto their Neighbour or Brethren know the Lord, the means of knowledge being placed so near as in the heart, so that all may know him from the least to the greatest and this knowledge is by and through the Son"* (L.N.21 p4).

God was *"the teacher of his people himself by and through the spirit of his son Jesus Christ"* (L.N. 17A p10).   All people should recognise that *"the divine Principle of Light and Life which comes by Jesus Christ is placed in the secret of every heart for our teacher and instructor"* (L.N.17A p6).   Writing to Elizabeth Wilson Joseph asserted that Christ would be *"a father unto thee, a teacher that cannot be removed into a corner, a leader that will lead thee in a path of safety in the strait and narrow way which will terminate in peace"* (L.N. 17A p10); and to Robert Walker *"thy eye will see thy teacher and as thou art concerned to obey it thou will be led in the path of true Judgement and experience that Baptism which rightly initiates into the Church of Christ. He that believeth and is baptized shall be saved"* (L.N.21 p4).

Accepting that Christ said to his disciples *"no man cometh to the Father but by me"* Joseph recognised that *"Christ in spirit is the leading way unto the Father"* (L.N.21 p4), he was indeed *"the alone way to God"* (L.N.22 p13).

The Grace of God was revealed to individuals who chose to follow *"the leadings of the Lord",* and it was this that supported them as they endeavoured to fulfil his *"requirings".* It was by Grace that they were preserved through regeneration, and, if they remained faithful, were kept unto salvation.

Joseph assured John Fearnley that the Grace of God existed *"in the secret of thine own heart, a sure and unerring guide that will never lead thee astray, it will preserve thee in the hour of temptation and lead thee in the way everlasting. It is a teacher which far exceeds the teachings of men, a faithful friend, a bosom companion that never did nor will consent to evil in any"* (L.N.10 p8).

The God Joseph believed in was not a remote deity. His was a personal God, a God who intervened in the lives of men. All events, experiences and conditions of life were explained *"as from God"* and *"as his will".* The many perplexing and distressing happenings of life were because *"the most high hath many ways of bringing poor man to the knowledge of himself"* (L.N.12 p11). These were to be accepted as part of the *"varied operations of his hand"* through which refinement of the soul was achieved. (L.N.7 p7)

In an individual's knowledge and experience of God, it was necessary above all else to love the Lord, for all his mercies and favours towards man *"what shall I render the Lord for all his benefits towards me for his great goodness and wonderful works who follows us from early in life and secretly preserves man from gross pollutions"* (L.N.8 p15). It was also necessary, however, to fear the

Lord *"for his mighty Power and his ability to both bless and blast every endeavour"* (L.N.12 p3) and an acceptance of the Lord's *"just judgements".* Describing to William Rhodes the nature of this *"pure holy fear"* Joseph wrote: *"fear him which is able to destroy both soul and body in hell".* He urged him to recognise that he should live in respectful awe of the Lord, as those who were his followers strive to do, for *"it is a fear that hath been their preservation in the hour of temptation which all are tryed with, and enabled them to know an overcoming through the power of Christ strengthening them"* and to accept that *"it is the fear that hath made many willing to leave all and follow him faithfully in the way of his leadings"* (L.N.33 p22).

Joseph expressed his understanding of the Fall of Man as *"the only way by which fallen Man can be restored unto the image of God, which our first Parents by disobeying his command and harkening to the voice of the enemy, lost; thus sin entered into the world, and since, mankind have been prone to evil, and by joining in therewith, are become the children of wrath"* (L.N.22 p18).

Deeply aware of man's sinful nature he accepted that *"all have sinned and fallen short of the Glory of God and we by nature are children of wrath, walking according to the Prince of the Power of air which worketh in the children of disobedience"* (L.N.22 p18). With his overwhelming concern for the destiny of an individual's soul, it was his belief that God was merciful and forgiving, and had *"placed a divine principle of light and life in Man which is able to counteract all the propensities of fallen nature"* (L.N.10 p7) and that he continually strove with man *"whilst he was wallowing in the mire and filth of sin by which alone he can experience reconciliation with his maker"* (L.N.10 p7).

In his infinite wisdom the Lord gave man his greatest gift, which was salvation. To attain salvation one had to *"forsake sin in all its appearances and cleave unto the Lord with full purpose of heart, for the eye hath not seen nor the ear heard neither hath it entered the heart of man to conceive the good things the Lord hath in store for those who love him above all, neither Grace nor Glory nor no good thing will be withheld from these in time or in eternity"* (L.N.10 p8).

All people had to recognise that the path to salvation lay in their acceptance of Christ, in whose name and power alone is salvation. To receive the Lord's gift of eternal life it was essential for each person to respond to *"the leadings of the Lord".* Joseph constantly urged people to give themselves "*wholly into the Lord's hand and be willing to do, and be just what he would have thee, then wilt thou receive in this world the hundredfold and in that which is to come everlasting life"* (L.N.14 p5).

"Seeing the Gospel which is the Power of God unto Salvation is Preached in all; those who are obedient thereunto shall be saved" (L.N.12 p6). The names of the saved were entered in *"the Lambs of Book of Life"* (L.N.33 p14). The fervent desire Joseph expressed to all that knew him was *"that you may be preserved with your eye single to the recompense of reward, so that ye may be able to fight the good fight and keep the faith and then do doubt not ye will experience the reward of all those who love his appearance, a crown of Glory which fadeth not away"* (L.N.12 p12).

Man experienced God when there was *"a waiting for the Lord"* in the secret of a person's heart. This could occur at any time, when an individual was alone or in the company of others, no designated place was required, no intermediary man was needed, no outward rites or rituals of man's devising were necessary, the worship of the Lord was not in preconceived or prescribed words. To become aware of *"the requirings"* or *"the breathings of the Lord"* a person must *"center into solemn silence ... and labour after that state of pure silence in which the Lord's still small voice is heard and distinctly understood"* (L.N.17A p6). This state of stillness and quietude of mind was necessary, as Joseph explained to Thomas Hold and Mark Brearer: *"so ye may know that he is God, feeling his awful presence near, to the breaking of your hearts, and contriting your spirits and enabling you to worship him who is a spirit in spirit and in truth"* (L.N.27 p51).

"I firmly believe his love is universally extended to the whole human race during the day of his visitation to them" (L.N.33 p14). This statement lay at the heart of Joseph's faith. He unceasingly urged people to *"prize the day of thy visitation".*

It was when one experienced *"the stirrings of the Lord"* and was aware of *"the breathings of the Lord"* that an individual came to some understanding of his or her state and that which was required of them. Men and women were given the choice as to whether or not they answered the call of the Lord. They did, however, have to accept responsibility for the decision taken, for *"they shall give account thereof on the day of judgement"* (L.N.26 p1). On *"the awful day when Inquisition for blood will be made"*, their decision would determine whether they were to be *"a companion for ever with the spirits of just men made Perfect through sufferings, or with him and suchlike who craved a drop of water to cool his tongue, being in great torment, and there for ever to remain"* (L.N.10 p10).

To those *"who hear and open unto him, he will come in and these will experience him to sit as a refiner with fire, For his Fan is in his hand, and if man resist not the operation of his power he will thoroughly purge the floor, that is cleanse the heart and make it fit for him to take up his abode in"* (L.N.15 p10). In a letter of encouragement to John Yeardley Joseph wrote: *"Thus would he make his visitations effectual unto thee in renewing and changing thy mind, weaning thee from the breast of the world and the enjoyment thereof, and enabling thee to enter into covenant with him who hath graciously visited thee"* (L.N. 21 p2). Those who responded to the visitations of the Lord were then separated out from the world as *"the Lords chosen people".*

It was vital then for an individual to preserve this state. The re-visitations of the Lord, if heeded, supported and maintained this process: *"therefore prize I beseech thee the day of thy visitation to use all diligence to make thy election sure, For I am certain thou has been called, the visitations of God's love hath been extended to thee"* (L.N.15 p12).

Without a positive response to *"a visitation",* there would be much potential danger to the soul. If rejected, however, the Lord continued to strive with that individual, though Joseph repeatedly warned people that should they continue to ignore the Lord then there might be a time when he would not come again and then the soul was lost for ever. He frequently pleaded that *"the day of thy visitation may not pass over thy head and thy portion be appointed with the unbelievers to all eternity"* (L.N.6 p38), or, as he wrote to Charles Smith: *"he willeth not the death of a sinner but had rather all should repent and live, by renewing his calls unto thee even when thou hast hardened thy heart against his reproofs; but I have been greatly afraid lest thou should reject the offers of his Love until he cease striving with thee and thou become a monument of his wrath"* (L.N.6 p18).

Man's understanding of God's intervention in the lives of individuals was incomplete. The requirement of each person was therefore to accept *"the Lord's dealings with them",* and with unquestioning faith to be prepared *"in that state of true quietude be willing to obey his voice"* (L.N.15 p5). Complete obedience to *"the manifestations of duty"* was demanded of those who wished to follow in the path of Truth, they were also to *"give up all and follow Christ that neither grace nor glory nor any good thing will be withheld"* (L.N.27 p19).

The will of man had to be subjugated so that the will of God would become dominant in daily living: *"thou may be concerned to wait for the renewings of that love which will strengthen thee to give up every thing that is inconsistent with the will of God and enable thee in sincerity to say; Not my will but thine O Lord be done in me and by me"* (L.N.8 p5). Joseph was convinced that it was *"not in Man that walketh to direct his own steps but a good mans steps are ordered by the Lord"* (L.N. 8 p3), and he continually insisted that there had to be a total submission of man's will to *"the Lords will", "the Lord's way"* and to *"the Lord's time".*

The preconditions for this were the renunciation of self, the giving up of the *"heart unto him without any reserve who will never accept a part of the whole"* (L.N.6 p38) and the seeking after and attaining *"to a state of true resignation".* Joseph urged everyone he encountered to *"wholly resign thyself into the Lords hands, to be even as passive clay in the hand of the potter that so his work may not be marred upon the wheel but then may be fashioned and formed by him into such a vessel as he in his wisdom may see meet, then will thou be enabled to bring forth fruit unto holiness"* (L.N.10 p1).

Being fully familiar with his own and others failings, Joseph recognized that compliance with the Lord's requirement of obedience was *"a great work and what we are not able to do for ourselves help is laid upon from one who is mighty to save and strong to deliver to the very uttermost"* (L.N.14 p1).

The ever-present threat of the Devil to the soul was keenly felt by Joseph, for whom it was *"necessary to keep up the warfare against him with spiritual weapons which will not be withheld from those who are concerned to gather unto the grace of God"* (L.N.33 p14). He was convinced that men and women could be *"strengthened to resist the Devil and cause him to flee"* (L.N.8 p5) through constant *"watchfulness, prayer"* and *"obedience to the requirings of the Lord".* It was then that they would experience *"the blessing of preservation"* and an overcoming of *"the unwearied enemy".* *"I am sensible of the frailty of human nature and the many baits and snares of that unwearied enemy we all have to war with who uses all his skill to keep us in the land of bondage. I am also sensible that there is one who is stronger than the strong armed man; who is able to cast him out and spoil his goods and set the oppressed seed at liberty to serve him"* (L.N.19 p19).

The Lord would help all who sought his assistance *"so I have oftens earnestly desired that thy obedience may keep pace with the knowledge he is pleased to favour thee with; and then thou will experience preservation in the hour of temptation"* (L.N.19 p7). A state of inward watchfulness was necessary, and compliance with *"the discipline which the most high hath been pleased to set as a hedge around us for our preservation"* (L.N.12 p3).

The lot of those who gave way to the temptations of the Devil was described to Elias Armitage thus: *"the enemy of mans happiness who continually watches our unwatchfulness; when he finds any off their guard lays baits and snares so subtilly, first by drawing up the mind after little things, and so as these are given way unto, they make room for greater temptations to enter until some are overtaken with those evils they would once have abhorr'd. Thy fall my friend is so great and by it thou has plunged thine own poor soul as into a gulph of misery, and perhaps now he who hath by his temptations drawn thee aside may be ready to vaunt thee and make thee believe he is sure of thee, for it will now be in vain to look unto the Lord for mercy for thou hast committed of the unpardonable sin against the Holy Ghost, and Hell must be thy portion"* (L.N.19 p2).

Believing, however, that God was merciful, Joseph urged Elias to *"wait with thy mouth in the dust, that so haply the Lord may be pleased to favour thee with Repentence"*, and also to *"patiently bear the indignation of the Lord, until he be pleased to arise and plead thy cause, the flaming sword turns every way and there is no other way for thee to experience restoration than by coming under it"*. He assured him that if he accepted he would come *"to praise and magnify the unmerited mercies of the Almighty that he did not cut thee off in thy disobedience, but gave thee space to repent"* (L.N.19 p2).

For those who had sinned it was essential, for the future state of their soul, that they looked for a reconciliation with God and sought his forgiveness through repentance for *"repentance is the gift of God when he is pleased to draw thee as by the cords of Love"* (L.N.8 p19). *"There is no way for man to experience reconciliation, but thro' sincere repentance for past transgressions, which implies a godly sorrow for sins of the past, and a humble walking before God for the time to come"* (L.N.26 p12). It was then, Joseph wrote, that *"in this humiliating state mans judgement is taken away his will is resigned to the divine will"* (L.N.33 p14) and he lived *"in true nothingness of self"* (L.N.8 p20).

It was through the work of divine Grace that sinful man was *"washed, stript and recloathed".* *"For Judgement must come over the transgressing nature before man can Praise the Lord for his mercies or sing the song of Moses and the Lamb, on the banks of deliverance"* (L.N.8 p19). Privations, trials, deep exercises and the temporary withdrawal of his presence were all part of the Lord's refining of the soul. *"I am fully persuaded if ever thou art again restored into favour with the Almighty it must be through deep sufferings"* (L.N.12 p8).

A *"second birth"* was required for those who wished *"to enter into that pure undefiled kingdom of rest and peace, into which none can come, but those who are regenerated and born again, and these experience all things to become new, new desires, new affections; the things in which they formally took delight becomes a great burden to them and instead of spending their precious time in unprofitable company their concern is to meditate in the Law of the Lord both day and night"* (L.N.15 p12). *"There is no other way for any to be his disciples, but by taking up their cross and denying self and following him in regeneration; experiencing the Lusts and affections to be crucified, and the inclinations changed, the mind redeemed from the spirit of the world and fixt upon those things which are above"* (L.N.10 p2). Those who had new Life brought by this second birth *"experienced being cleansed by the spirit of Judgement and burning and a feeling the Lord to be with them heartily engaged in his cause"* (L.N.10 p7).

The life, deeds and words of every individual would be

judged on *"the great day of account* for *the Lord is our Judge. Remembering that we are accountable to the most high for every neglected opportunity put into our hand"* (L.N.33 p4). The *"more thou hast been favoured with the greater will be thy condemnation if thou art not bringing forth fruit answerable thereunto"* (L.N.6 p18).

Joseph expressed his belief in the judgement of the Lord and the consequences for those that failed to respond to his call to follow him in very clear, unequivocal language: *"Sin must never go unpunished let it be of what kind it may"* (L.N.8 p5). Describing the fate of the wilfully disobedient he issued a severe warning to Charles Smith: *"if thou art not thoroughly separated from thy sins but art keeping those things alive that thy natural inclination is most prone unto, the Language unto you will be I know thee not thou worker of iniquity and how awful will the prospect be if thou should see Abraham, Isaac and Jacob and all the Prophets and faithful servants of Jesus in the Kingdom and thyself shut out"* (L.N.6 p12). Writing to Benjamin Beever he cautioned: *"the awful consequence of living in sin, the punishment of which is eternal death, to be tormented with the Devil and his Angels in the lake that burneth with fire and Brimstone* (L.N.22 p18). His fervent message to others was this: *"if you live in sin and die in the same we cannot enter the kingdom of heaven"* (L.N.10 p7).

Joseph continually sought to explain that those who committed themselves to the Lord's way would experience his *"undefiled kingdom of rest and peace"* here on earth. His advice to Charles Unsworth was this: *"it certainly is therefore the greatest wisdom and the only way to a solid happiness in this life, to seek the kingdom of God, and his righteousness, in the first place and this can only be in those seasons when he is pleased to renew the visitations of his love unto us"* (L.N.17 p17). It was his belief that *"the Lord's People experience the kingdom of heaven to be come, and at times are favoured to know a sitting in the heavenly places in Christ Jesus"* (L.N.15 p7). It was then that one could experience *"the mysteries of that Kingdom which stands not in outward observations but in righteousness, peace and joy in the Holy Ghost"* (L.N.33 p20).

The reward for a life truly lived in the love and fear of the Lord in which one's duty in obedience to *"the requirings of the Lord"* had been fulfilled were the words *"well done thou good and faithful servant"* (L.N.6 p12) and admittance into the heavenly kingdom and life everlasting.

Joseph was acutely aware that death, came in a *"time not our own".* It was imperative, therefore, that everyone prepared for their *"final Change",* the time of their *"dissolution",* for *"none of us know how or after what manner we may be called from works to rewards"* (L.N.10 p9). Following the unexpected death of Charles Ives he wrote: *"when we leave our habitations we know not that we must ever return to them again, when we go to Bed we know not that we must ever arise, when we fall asleep we know not that we must ever open our eyes until we open them in Eternity"* (L.N.13 p17).

The Scriptures were central to Joseph's faith, for in them he found the word of God as spoken by the Prophets, Jesus Christ and his Apostles. Expressing to Henry Swire his gratitude for this knowledge, he wrote: *"How profitably instructing and encouraging to faithfulness are the remarks recorded in the scriptures of Truth, when opened up to us in the newness of Life. May thou my friend never seek to comprehend them in the natural understanding, ... but dwell deep with the seed which lieth low thus will the mysteries contained therein be opened unto thee in the Lords way and time to thy humbling admiration"* (L.N.15 p17).

The lives of the Prophets and the Apostles were important to him as they were individuals through whom God worked his purposes. In a letter of encouragement to Enoch Dickinson he commented: *"It hath been instructive and encouraging to my mind, when I have read the Scriptures of truth, how wonderfully the Lord wrought the deliverance of his People formerly through weak instruments"* (L.N.12 p7).

A belief in the supernatural was part of Joseph's spiritual life. It was understood that God, on occasions, revealed himself and his purposes through visions and dreams. The importance that these had for Joseph is reflected in the number he recorded in his Notebooks.

In 1784 Joseph wrote an account of such a vision and the effect this had on him. *"I thought I saw myself in a Beautiful meadow in the company with J: S: and W: T: to intimate friends of mine whose prosperity in the truth I think I desire as my own, on the South side of this meadow run a broad River, and on the North a small brook like a millstream, which met together at the bottom or East end, at the West end was a good dwelling house, whilst we were walking in this beautiful field, I perceived a Storm to arise in the West and I told my companions thereof, intreating them to flee with me for our lives: one of them seem'd to be quite insensible of the approaching dangers and resolutely determined to have his own will and way turning a deaf ear to all intreaties; the other appeared in some measure to be sensible of our precarious situation but harkening to the words of the former his eyesight for a season became dim, The River began to rise very fast and I tarried until it was got to the brink, and then fled in Sorrow of heart to leave my dear friends behind into the house at the West end of the meadow, imagining I should be safe there but after I had been there a little while I considered the house was only built by man and therefore would not be able to withstand the flood which appeared as if it would drive down all before it, The Water began to enter therein and I got out as speedily as possible I could, not knowing where to go. I stood still a little, and then lifting up my eyes saw a little from the East end of the House a high Rock, the brook running upon the north side thereof, upon which I got and found upon the south side a piece of ground which appeared to be quite firm and covered with grass, I stepped thereon, but soon found by mistake it giving way and it was with great difficulty I got my feet again upon the Rock, when looking to see for the meadow where I had left my companions it was entirely swept away then turning my Eye a little I saw standing close to me on my left side one of them (vis) W: T: We rejoiced greatly to see each other and that we were on a safe place almost surrounded with a flood on every side, whilst we saw many others swept away in the general deluge. What became of my other companion I know not for I saw him no more. I saw likewise many others upon the Rock some of whom are now living in the Body, and among the rest a Woman an intimate acquaintance of mine, who notwithstanding I shewed her the danger, could not prevent her from going to stand upon the earth at the south side of the rock, which gave way with her and I saw her no more, I then awoke, and slept no more this night and being under a close engagement of Spirit that whatsoever I had to pass thro' my feet might be firmly established upon Christ the Rock and true foundation of every righteous generation and then altho' the wins may blow, the rains descend and floods beat against me I shall experience preservation"* (J.W. Misc. Papers).

THE MINISTRY OF JOSEPH WOOD

It was during 1778, at the age of twenty-eight, that Joseph first began to feel the Lord's requirement for him to speak in public. The first reference to *"I dropt a few words"* occurs during a Visit to the Families of Friends of High Flatts Meeting (S.N.12 p5).

One year later the Elders and other Ministers of High Flatts Meeting affirmed that it was "in the twenty ninth year of his age was his first appearance in the Ministry, in great fear and brokenness of spirit" (J.W. Testimony Pontefract Mo.Mg.).

The position of a Quaker Minister was unlike that of the ordained Minister in other non-conformist congregations or the Priest within the established Church since it was not invested with any ministerial or pastoral authority. For fellow-believers a man or woman so recognised was accepted as one of those people through whom the word of God was made known, His will being revealed in the spoken word. The Elders of the Meeting were those who were entrusted with responsibilities associated with the spiritual state of members, and the Overseers undertook the organisation of the affairs of the Meeting.

There were those during the Quietist years who were fearful of a call to ministry and were deeply concerned "they might outrun their Guide and speak out of turn". This, however, meant that when "once the outward compulsion had become irresistable, peace of mind was only to be obtained by faithful obedience whatever the cost or inconvenience" (Thistlethwaite).

After receiving news that Joseph had appeared in ministry, his friend, Joseph King, of Glasshouses near Newcastle, wrote to him: "I was rejoiced to be informed of thy becoming a fruiting Branch it is what I foresometime Past expected would be thy happy lott" (J.W. Misc. Papers).

Joseph laboured unceasingly, proclaiming the word of the Lord to all who would listen urging them to seek salvation through the Lord's redeeming love. His proven ability to set forth the truths of gospel love and to explain in language that his hearers understood is evidenced in the countless numbers of people who responded to his call. "The list of his converts were legion" (Mills) and included men and women of every age, position in life, the educated and the illiterate, the prosperous and the less fortunate. The impact of his message profoundly affected those who encountered him as he preached in a public Meeting or gathering or when he shared the intimate experience of "an opportunity" in the privacy of a home. In like manner the numerous recipients of his many letters were no less powerfully influenced. Acknowledging their response, he then embarked on what he understood to be a major task of his ministering "duty", this being to participate in their daily lives in order to support and enrich their faith. He was seen by them as bearing a responsibility in spiritual matters, and accordingly they allowed him to enter their lives.

Joseph was a powerful, persuasive and "eminently gifted preacher". For those who heard him he spoke "not with the enticing words of man's wisdom but in demonstration of the Spirit and of power" (J.W. Testimony Pontefract Mo. Mg.). Such would have been the experience of those who attended a public meeting appointed for Joseph at Low Bentham in 1818, of which John Yeardley wrote: "A pretty many who usually attend meetings, and

David Butler

Ministers' Stand
Low Bentham Meeting House

a great concourse of people of other societies, attended, so that the meeting house, both above and below stairs, was well filled, and several were in the passage and in an adjoining room" (Tylor).

Joseph consistently used several descriptions for his spoken ministry, such as *"I had a few words", "I had a long time", "I had a pretty long time", "I had a very long time", "I had a very open time", "I was pretty largely opened", "having several short communications as matter opened", "I was very much enlarged in testimony therein".* His testimony was delivered *"to the tendering of many hearts, to the peace to my own mind".*

After a Meeting at Shoebroad having delivered testimony *"for a long time"* and then having *"had a few words more",* he wrote: *"I may say my mind was bow'd in humble thanksgiving before the most high for this days peculiar favour"* (S.N.16 p8).

Following a Meeting in Pontefract he recorded that he had had: *"for some time a concern upon my mind to attend their first day meetings and I was glad I gave up thereto, for tho' my exercise therein was heavy, and I had very close doctrine to deliver to some states, yet I was favoured with strength fully to relieve my mind, and I believe it was a season of renewed favour to many"* (L.N.30 p10).

Joseph was fearful to stand and speak until he felt it was right to do so, for he was not "forward to offer his gift, patiently abiding in the deep till he felt the holy fire burn" (J.W. Testimony Pontefract Mo.Mg).   On many occasions he recorded that he waited until the leadings of the Spirit arose in his heart: *"After a considerable time in silence, I stood up in much weakness, but feeling the exercise of my Gift a gradual increase in strength, I was enabled to bear a long testimony to the Truth, opening in a convincing manner the way of Life and salvation, through Jesus christ the mediator of the everlasting covenant from Rom: C: 5. v: 8,9"* (L.N.30 p14).   At a Meeting the following month, *"I was very poor and low in the forepart thereof, but a little matter opening, I stood up pretty soon, in great weakness, not expecting to have much to say, but to my humbling admiration, Life arose gradually, and with the increased strength, I was able to bear a very long testimony from 2 Thess: C: 3. v: 5"* (L.N.30 p17).   After a Meeting at High Flatts he recorded: "*a very weighty exercise came over my mind and soon after I sat down therein the word was as a fire in my bones and I was early constrained to stand upon my feet*" (S.N.51 p1).

Joseph felt intensely the need of spiritual, emotional and physical fortitude that was required when speaking "*gospel truth*", and at times this weighed heavily upon him. After attending a Meeting near Oldham he noted: *"I expected I had fully cleared myself before and that I might be favoured to sit in silence amongst them, but found it to the contrary, being largely opened amongst them to various states from Jonah C: 1. v: 2"* (S.N.35 p3).

He frequently recorded that he had spoken *"to some states present"* that is, to those in various conditions, spiritual and temporal. Amongst these would be *"the youth"*, "*those with* children in their care", "servants", "the bereaved", "the aged", "the poor in spirit", "the unexperienced", "those under convincement", the "newly convinced", the "worldly minded raw people", "steady valuable friends" and "those of a tryed tempted state". Those who had heard his and others' words in a Meeting were described as being "much tendered" or "in much brokenness".

Rarely did he note the response of an individual, though he did after a Meeting, called by Job Thomas, in Llweynduin, Wales: "after meeting a sober Woman came to Job in much tenderness and told him, she was greatly affected under my appearances, altho' she understood not a word I said" (S.N.22 p7).

Though there are no eye-witness accounts of Joseph's looks, bearing and voice when delivering public testimony, several of his hearers recorded the impact of his words. John Yeardley, having heard Joseph preach at a public meeting in Middlestown, wrote that "it was the most extraordinary time I have ever knew. My friend bore a long and powerful testimony to the tendering of many present. If I ever forget it while in my natural senses I fear I will be losing my habitation in the truth for it was as if Heaven opened and the Most High poured down his Blessed spirit in an unbounded degree" (Tylor). Elizabeth Yeardley also remembered Joseph's powers as a preacher when on a visit to Westmorland and Lancashire: "J.W. was very much favoured all the time he was in those parts. He really appears endowed with astonishing powers" (Bower and Knight).

After an unnamed Yorkshire Quaker had encountered Joseph speaking during a visit to Dudley, he wrote to him: "forgive me if, for a few moments, I trespass upon your candour and patience. I never felt myself more completely elevated above the fashionable vanities of this world than by your truly Christian and apostolic address. The impression which it has left upon my mind is greater than anything I ever before experienced. May that impression be deep, solid and lasting! I shall have cause to recollect with feelings of the liveliest gratitude the day which brought me acquainted with such a man" (L.N.32 p22).

The wife of a Clergyman described to her friend in London how her daughter had heard Joseph preach at Melbourne in Derbyshire: *"she says never in her Life, did she hear anything at all to equal him, either in manner (which was truly solemn) or matter, the doctrine she says was wholly scriptural, every person in the Chapel seemed greatly affected, and some even to extreme agitation"* (L.N.34 p20).

The seclusion of *"an opportunity"* taking place in a home offered a more personal and confidential setting for a spiritual encounter. The nature of such an occasion varied according to whether it was when two individuals came together or it was shared by several people.

The after dinner *"family opportunity"* was an essential part of life at Newhouse. Such a *"setting"* was recorded by Joseph: *"after we had read as usual our minds were sweetly comforted with a solemn quietude and towards the close of the opportunity I had a pretty long testimony to bear"* (L.N.20 p6). Visiting friends were invited to sit with the family, as on the occasion when Mary Rotherford and Catharine Tricket were paying a religious visit to the families of Friends of High Flatts Meeting. In his account of this evening gathering Joseph wrote: *"The opportunity in our family was mercifully covered with an awful solemnity, and under the pure influence of Gospel Love caution counsel advice and encouragement were plentifully communicated suitable to our various states"* (S.N.23 p7).

The time spent by the family of Christiana Hustler of Undercliffe and several Friends, during which Joseph and John Bottomley had testimony and prayer, was recorded by Joseph as: *"the precious opportunity together in which we were favoured to partake of the sheddings abroad of that divine Love which nearly unites the Lords children together"* (S.N.21 p11). During the time his friend Timothy Sykes was staying with him Joseph recorded how as the two of them: *"set together in My Parlour we closed into silence, the divine Power mercifully overshadowing us, my spirit was bowed and tendered before the most high and I had a pretty long testimony to bear to the Truth from 2 Cor: C: 10. v: 4,5"* (L.N.24 p13). Following the burial of his friend George Chapman, Joseph noted: *"I had a pretty long testimony to bear to his son in which I had caution, counsel and encouragement to communicate to him, and afterwards had a short but encouraging testimony to his widow from Jer: C: 49. v: 11"* (L.N.31 p16). Describing his convert John Yeardley of Blacker, Joseph recorded that *"he was convinced of the Truth in an opportunity I had at his Father's house"* (L.N.20 p4).

For Joseph and his hearers the words spoken in worship were divine in origin, arising from the immediate promptings of *"the Inward Light of Christ"* and uttered in the name of the Lord. Accordingly these could in no way be prepared prior to the time of worship or composed to a set of liturgical rules and conventions. For this reason Joseph was very ready in his condemnation of the preaching of the *"hireling priest"* heard by those attending *"the Steeplehouse"*. He rejected the *"lifeless ministry exercised in the will and wisdom of the creature"* (S.N.61 p23) as part of *"an empty profession"* and disputed the validity of *"the outward forms of worship"* shaped by man's ideas acquired from learning. He continually challenged the *"formal Preaching, praying and singing and other things which they look upon as religious duties, performed in their own will, way or time without waiting to feel his spirit to lead them into these services, which alone can render them acceptable unto him and truly profitable one unto another"* (L.N.27 p14). One of the rare occasions when he gave details of his testimony he wrote that it was his aim: *"to show the difference betwixt the true and false ministries, and the inconsistency with the Gospel dispensation of sending one to academys to learn to preach as other people go apprentice to learn trades and then sell it unto the people contrary to the command of Christ who when he sent forth his disciples said unto them Freely ye have received freely give"* (S.N.60 p17).

Rooted deeply in the Scriptures, Joseph's faith found expression through the constant use of biblical references. His preaching was therefore based on the word of God as spoken by the Prophets, Christ and the Apostles. "He was often favoured in an extraordinary manner to explain to the people Scripture Truth; and his ministry on these occasions was often attended with the powerful blazing influence of the spirit to the convincement of many" (J.W. Testimony Pontefract Mo.Mg.). He always recorded the passage of Scripture that strengthened and supported the words that *"opened"* to him but what he actually said was very rarely noted. In like manner a record of Biblical quotations used by others was kept.

 Endowed with this ability to clearly open scriptural truth which gave inspiration and guidance to assembled Friends, Joseph was readily welcomed into the Meetings he visited. Having encountered the man and heard his stirring message, members then wished for him to return and continue his service to them.

From Macclesfield, Samuel Stonehewer wrote to Joseph: "whilst I am wrighting it is with me to inform thee our meeting is still rather on the incrise and think if thou was at liberty or thought it right to favour us with thy company by way of a friendly visit, thou would be pleased to see some of us and we should as we always was much pleased to see thee thinking it a verry long while since thou or dear J.B. was our way" (J.W. Misc. Papers). After Joseph had attended a Meeting at Selston near Mansfield, Daniel Sutton wrote to him urging him to pay them another visit for "we believe our neighbours and others have been more open and unprejudiced towards us since your journey this way" (J.W. Misc.Papers).

It is clear that even those *"not in profession with us"* held

Joseph in high regard as a preacher. This is particularly evident in his dealings with the many people whose Chapels or Meeting Houses he was allowed to use for public meetings for worship. Writing to Samuel Laver, Joseph stated: *"I have no desire to draw People from one Profession of Religion to another yet I have an earnest desire that all might come up faithful in obedience to the manifestations they are favoured with"* (L.N.19 p11). It is apparent, however, that having heard Joseph's gospel ministry members of the Established Church, Methodists, Presbyterians and others who *"were dissatisfied"* sought him out as someone with whom they could share their misgivings and doubts in confidence and from whom they knew they would receive honest, straight advice and guidance. This frequently resulted in them attending Meetings, and for some, spending time with Joseph at Newhouse. For many *"a convincement in the Truth"* followed. "He was especially helpful to such as the Lord was gathering from the barren mountains of an empty profession to the knowledge of the truth, and he was frequent, in solemn supplication for these and for the awakening of those who were at ease in Zion" (J.W. Testimony Pontefract Mo.Mg.).

For Joseph regular attendance at both First Day (Sunday) and Week Day Meetings was essential, a foremost requirement of those who believed in Quaker Truth. This he considered to be of the utmost importance to both the life of an individual believer and the Meeting to which he or she belonged. He explained to the family of William Read: *"when I was Hearty I did not think the 1st. day of the Week well spent if I did not get to some Meeting"* (S.N.3 p2). It was with a determined persistence that he spoke and wrote of this religious duty for "He was concerned to impress on the minds of his friends the necessity of a due attendance of weekday meetings, believing that such as were negligent in this duty never experienced an attainment to the state of strong men in truth" (J.W. Testimony Pontefract Mo.Mg.).

In order to fulfil his duty as a minister of the gospel, Joseph commenced his lifelong commitment to visiting First Day, Week Day, Monthly, Quarterly and Yearly Meetings of the Society of Friends. However, unlike many of his contemporaries, who as part of their religious duty travelled abroad, Joseph's journeyings were limited. When describing his ministry to Charles Unsworth he wrote: *"I am not one of those that would compass Sea or Land to gain proselytes"* (L.N.33 p4). Later to John Yeardley he declared: *"I can honestly appeal to him who knoweth the secrets of every heart that I have nothing in view in all my religious movements, but the peace to my own mind I neither seek for, nor expect great things for myself, or look for great things to arise from my labours; but if the precious life is but preserved for a prey it will be enough"* (L.N.27 p18).

Travelling throughout counties previously visited Joseph extended his journeyings to include Northumberland, Staffordshire, Shropshire, Hertfordshire, Buckinghamshire, Norfolk, Cambridgeshire and Lincolnshire. Interestingly, he only once recorded having made the journey to London. This was undertaken in 1775 in order to attend the London Yearly Meeting (S.N. 5).

It was during these journeys that he saw at first hand the state and circumstances of numerous Quaker Meetings, some of which varied from his own. Participating in the worship and work of these he witnessed the realities of both local and national Quakerism. From this experience he gained a clear understanding of the day-to-day workings of the Society and the importance of the guiding influence of the Yearly Meeting.

At many of the gatherings he came into contact with leading *"Publick Friends and Strangers"* of his day, some of whom he came to know well, enjoying lifelong friendships with them. These were the eminent and highly respected men and women who, as *"travelling friends",* devoted themselves, their time and energies to visiting Meetings. From their accounts of the Lord's dealings with them and their many testimonies and exhortations Joseph undoubtedly received spiritual sustenance.

Close and lasting contacts were also established with those attending his own Meeting and with the members of the many Meetings he went to regularly, mutual visiting and letter-writing becoming an important part of these. Setting forth the value of faithful religious friendships, he described these to Charles Unsworth as *"one of the greatest blessings we can be favoured with in life",* explaining to him that *"if one cool his zeal to God the other endeavours to increase a warmth in him by timely advice or admonition. Or if one thro' unwatchfulness falls the other is ready to lend a helping hand"* (L.N.33 p5). Such a friendship was exemplified in his relationship with John Bottomley, who, before becoming the Overseer of the woods of the Bosville Estate, had been, for many years, a servant in his household. Unequal in their social standing, they were equals in their gospel ministries. John went with Joseph to countless Meetings and accompanied him on numerous journeys to their mutual satisfaction. To Susanna Dickinson he wrote: *"there is nothing that manifests the sincerity of any ones friendship more, than if we see anything approaching, that our friend may be likely to suffer loss by; than faithfully warning them of the danger"* (L.N.19 p8).

Joseph considered that anyone who could not read suffered a great disadvantage. Such a person was deprived of the opportunity to read the Scriptures, the record of God's dealings with man at first hand, and so had little understanding of the will of the Lord and his redeeming love.

This conviction prompted him to give instruction to a number of young men, believing that the ability to read well would be of benefit to them in both their religious life and everyday living.

The lessons were held at Newhouse after First Day Meeting and on weekday evenings. Frequently *"the scholar"* would stay the night in readiness for the following day's work. Success was recognized when passages from the Scriptures could be read. The scholars were also involved in copying religious tracts, epistles and letters which Joseph wished to share with Friends. His desire that the Bible be available to all may also account for his support of those in the neighbourhood who were associated with the work of the British and Foreign Bible Society. Amongst the surviving Miscellaneous Papers there is printed material from the Society to members.

J. Travis Mills was aware of Joseph and the surviving Notebooks. In his book, published in 1935, John Bright and the Quakers, of Joseph Wood he wrote: "In holiness of life, in unquenchable zeal for the spread of Truth, and for the salvation of individual souls, he was surpassed by few in his day. His was a small orbit, but within its range he showed once more that holy courage triumphant over every weakness of the flesh and spirit which was so conspicuous a characteristic of the early Quakers, and which through ages has never been left without witness among their spiritual sons".

Local Meetings Houses visited by Joseph Wood

Wooldale Meeting House

1812

1771

Paddock Meeting House,
Huddersfield

David Butler

64

Brighouse
Meeting
House

Todmorden
Meeting
House

Leeds Meeting House

David Butler

THE WRITINGS OF JOSEPH WOOD

The full extent of Joseph's writings is not known, but it is clear that throughout the years of his ministry he meticulously recorded the events of his daily life and work as a Minister of the gospel, and the correspondence he wrote and received.

In their book *Plain Country Friends, The Quakers of Wooldale, High Flatts and Midhope* David Bower and John Knight wrote of Joseph's writings that "his fifty-five year long Journals and Correspondence has never been published and have remained virtually unknown outside his descendents' family circle. In Joseph Wood the Religious Society of Friends had its own Samuel Pepys. Quite possibly his detailed record of Quaker life between 1767 - 1821 is unrivalled".

Joseph's undoubted commitment to his writing is clearly evidenced in the surviving Notebooks, as is his acceptance of the continuous application and discipline necessary to carry out this self commissioned task. It was his belief that the Truths spoken at the Meetings he attended, the opportunities he took part in and the issues raised in his memoranda and letters should be available for the enlightenment and support of others who might read them.

He expressed his intentions: *"As I have apprehended there may be a service in leaving to posterity some remarks of such of my acquaintance as have thro' their diligent attention and Obedience to the Grace of God been preserved in a religious course of Life and been an honour to the Truth they profess that others may be encouraged to receive and believe the same principle of Light and Life which comes by Jesus Christ. So I believe it may be equally as serviceable to leave some remarks concerning those who thro' unwatchfulness have suffered the light in them to become darkness and so have been walking they knew not where, that others may thereby learn to hear and fear lest they fall in the hour of temptation and by forsaking the true light follow him whose work is to deceive"* (L.N.6 p6). To Charles Smith he wrote: *"I remark this with a view that it may be a means of stirring up some who may read it when I may be laid in the silent Grave, not to rest satisfied in the profession that so they may be good examples unto those who may be enquiring the way to Zion, that their lights may so shine before men that those who behold their good works the product of living Faith may be made to magnify the Principle we profess"* (L.N.6 p11).

Joseph's writings can conveniently be divided into Memoranda, Accounts of Journeys, Accounts of Meetings, Letters and Selected Quaker Writings.

Memoranda

The entries Joseph made in his memoranda offer insights into the main events in his life as a minister of the gospel. It is not clear if he regarded entries as complete in themselves or whether he intended the contents as aides-memoir, as was often the practice, for a more detailed diary. The surviving memoranda are found in the Large Notebooks 16-20, 23-25, 28-32, 34-37.

Joseph recorded his regular attendance at First Day, Week Day and Monthly Meetings held at High Flatts, Wooldale, Burton (Barnsley), Lumbroyd (Penistone), Wakefield, Agbrigg and Dewsbury. He noted those who attended the Meetings, and those who stood in testimony, supplication and exhortation and offered prayer and praises. The state of the Meetings and how long they lasted was also recorded. He gave account of his companions, the houses they called at and the hostelries in which they took refreshment and overnight accommodation.

Much of Joseph's time and energy were spent making visits to neighbours and Friends. While he enjoyed the social aspects of these visits, they provided him with the opportunity to aid the spiritual well-being of those he met. The names of those visited are all recorded, although only rarely did he note the nature of the support, encouragement or advice he offered or of the warnings he gave.

Part of the Index of Memoranda   Large Notebook 29

On occasions when the Elders of the Meeting or an individual expressed a particular *"concern"* relating to members, *"a Visiting of Families of Friends"* was undertaken. Such visits included those of a religious and general pastoral nature - to *"those with the care of the young",* to *"those negligent in due attendance of meetings"* and to *"those disowned but continue to attend meetings".*   Joseph participated in many such visits, noting in great detail those who had been visited, the Friends who had gone with him, the nature of the opportunities which occurred, the advice and guidance offered and the reception received.   These accounts demonstrate the commitment needed for such an enterprise, which would last over many days, and the very considerable demands that fell on those undertaking the visit.

Joseph was willing to accompany other Friends when they undertook a visit in response to *"a concern".*   This could be to members of certain Meetings within a stated Monthly Meeting, or to groups of people they felt were in need of spiritual guidance, such as the prisoners in the House of Correction in Wakefield.

With his great friend Thomas Shillitoe of Barnsley, he went on a religious visit to the Public Houses in Barnsley and its neighbourhood and also visited the families of those Luddities who were hanged at York Castle.

Thomas Shillitoe 1754- 1836

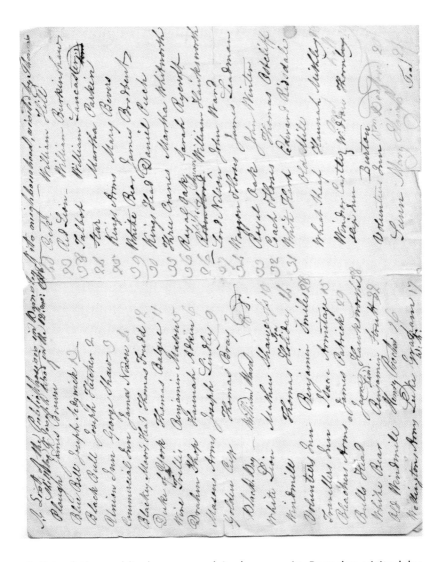

A list of the public houses and innkeepers in Barnsley visited by Thomas Shillitoe and Joseph Wood in the 12ᵗʰ mo. 1816

(J.W. Misc. Papers)

An account of the premature death of a youth is but one example of the numerous entries concerned with unexpected tragic incidents. Joseph elicited from such warnings *"how necessary it is for us to be at all times ready for our final change, seeing that we know not how soon or how suddenly he who hath given us Life Breath and being may call us to resign the same"* (L.N.23 p9).

Joseph meticulously recorded the Subscription lists for monies raised in connection with the building, rebuilding, enlarging and buying of Meeting Houses and for the relief of those suffering the consequences of war. These included the names, residences and Meetings of all those listed.

Many entries related to the marriages and burials of Friends who attended his own and other Meetings. They included details of the arrangements made for these occasions, the names of those involved and a description of the gathering.

From his many accounts of thunderstorms it is clear that Joseph had a great fear of such happenings. Describing these in detail, he was concerned not only with the occurrence itself but with the damage to property and personal injury. He was also mindful to record that mere chance or luck had no place in natural events, within *"a most awful and tremendous Thunderstorm"* the hand of Providence was revealed.

In one such case, he noted the he had *"not heard of any damage anywhere done this day"* and *"no one received the least harm"* and expressed his relief at this: *"how wonderfully did the interposition of kind providence appear"* (L.N.28 p7); On occasions when buildings were destroyed and *"life was despaired of"* his plea was *"O that these solemn warnings may be a means of awakening sinners to repentance, and cause all so to number their days as to apply their hearts unto Wisdom"* (L.N.25 p2).

Accounts of Journeys

"Quakers' Path", North Ings near Commondale on Joseph's route
between Castleton and Guisborough

From 1767 to his death in 1821 Joseph embarked on journeys
in order to fulfil what he regarded as a major obligation of his
religious duty, his attendance at Meetings. The accounts of the
journeys are found in the Small Notebooks, (except 2 and 18)
and in the Large Notebooks 20, 23-25, 28-30, 32, 34-37.

It was not unusual for many weeks to pass between the
time when Joseph had "*a concern*" to embark on a journey and
the journey itself, be it a local or extended one. It was of the
utmost importance to him that such an undertaking was not
commenced prematurely, "*having a prospect for a considerable
time of paying a religious visit to the inhabitants of Ing Birchworth
and the neighbourhood thereof waiting patiently until I apprehended*

the time was clearly pointed out to me" (S.N.61 p22).

Joseph travelled on foot in all weather conditions irrespective of the state of the roads, tracks and pathways. He often noted the miles walked, frequently twenty to thirty miles in a day. On many occasions he had to walk such distances on several consecutive days.

It was indeed a rare occasion when Joseph rode a horse. During a journey a horse might be offered by a fellow Friend and others in the company willingly accepted such an offer, but Joseph would decline, preferring to walk. It was not until his health began to deteriorate seriously and bouts of sickness and *"of being unwell"* were noted that this changed or he accepted a seat in a Friend's chaise or gig.

As he grew older, Joseph found walking more difficult, as on the day he went to Wakefield to visit the prisoners in the House of Correction: *"I travelled slowly, feeling the infirmities of advancing years increasing upon me and more so through long continuance of bodily indisposition. The day was also wet, and the roads very dirty, so that I travelled in great weariness of body, yet had no cause to complain, being helped along the way beyond my expectation"*

(S.N.60 p11).

In the winter months, in order to take advantage of the daylight, he began many of the journeys in the early hours of the morning. On occasions he noted that, when setting out or arriving at Meeting a friend accompanied him with *"a Lanthorn"*. The hour of his return home was always recorded and sometimes, after an extended journey, he remarked his contentment at once again being at Newhouse and his relief that *"all was well", "all were in good health",* noting, too, the family's pleasure at seeing him *"returned safely".*

It is clear that he had time to enjoy his surroundings, for

frequently he commented on the terrain and the view, expressing his delight in hills, moorland, valleys, rivers and streams, things which *"caused me many times to admire the wonderful work of him who made the heavens and earth, the seas and the fountains of water"* (S.N.26 p2). He found time to visit castles and country estates, to descend into Peak Cavern in Derbyshire, to take the waters in Harrogate and to bathe in the sea at Scarborough and Whitby. While visiting Jacob Bright in Rochdale he went after dinner *"to look thro' their cotton factory in which 200 hands are employed; the many different kinds of machinery at work was a curiosity to us who had seen nothing of the kind before"* (Mills). Similarly when on his way to the Welsh Yearly Meeting at Newtown, Montgomeryshire whilst staying in the vicinity of Coalbrookdale he was equally intrigued at the working of the iron foundry owned by the Darby family. *"Friend Birchall and me took a walk amongst the Iron works which to me was a great curiosity"* (S.N.4 p5).

Hugely important to Joseph were the people who accompanied him on his journeys. He derived great pleasure and much personal and spiritual support from the fellowship of those with whom he was uniting in a shared purpose. He always noted the name of the person who was *"my companion this Journey".* It was not unusual for his companion's house to be the first call of the day where breakfast was taken. At other times Joseph would provide overnight accommodation for his companion before the day of departure. It was also frequently the custom that after making a visit to a Meeting or to a Friend's house someone would escort him several miles *"and then return'd".*

If the journey was an extended one, the companion often agreed to accompany him throughout. There were, however, many occasions when this was not the case. It was then customary for a member of one of the Meetings Joseph attended or from one of the families with whom he had lodged to accompany him to the next place. The setting-out on a return journey would commonly be described as occurring *"in the company of many friends",* those taking the same direction travelling together. When the purpose of the journey was to attend one of the major Society gatherings, Joseph and his companion would join others on the road.

On certain occasions this created a large group of distinctly recognisable travellers. Joseph's meticulous record of the names of those who regularly joined with him is evidence of the numbers of Friends who, like him, understood it to be part of their spiritual life to attend local and county-wide Meetings.

During such journeys, if Joseph needed accommodation, he would frequently stay at the home of a local Friend. To be made welcome in this way was always greatly appreciated, particularly when the weather had been bad: *"we were kindly and affectionately received and great care taken of us being both wet and weary"* (S.N.24 p3).

Along the routes taken by Joseph and his friends were inns and hostelries at which they regularly took refreshment and also lodgings. He recorded in great detail the places, the names of the houses and the amounts of money that were paid for liquor, for brandy or rum and water, a pint of ale or porter, for eating, for breakfast, dinner and supper. On some occasions, however, it was not necessary to break his journey in this way, *"having dined upon the road of provisions I brought with me from home"* (S.N.60 p11).

The quality of the accommodation was frequently commented on as was the reception by the Innkeeper. When the Landlord was amenable religious pamphlets were frequently distributed. At times, when a number of Quakers stayed overnight Joseph recorded that, if the Landlord was agreeable, they took a room and held "*an opportunity*" together.

Accounts of Meetings

Ye Quakers Meeting
Illustration from the cover of Small Notebook 27

"In the course of his religious labours, he visited the meetings of Friends generally in most of the Quarterly Meetings of England and many meetings within the principality of Wales, and divers of them repeatedly" (J.W. Testimony Pontefract Mo.Mg.).

Meetings were important to Joseph because, as he wrote to Joshua Roberts: *"Now they that feared the Lord formerly met often together so they do to this day they dare not neglect their duty in this whatever their situation in life may be"* (L.N.8 p6).

John Yeardley, one of his converts, gives an insight into Joseph's established habit of keeping detailed records of Meetings he attended: *"On his return home from services he would spend the day in an upper room, without a fire even in the severest weather, writing a minute account of all that had happened"* (Tylor).

The accounts of such Meetings were inevitably similar, in as much as what took place followed a consistent pattern according to the type of Quaker gathering. Joseph recorded First Day and Week Day Meetings and those held during Monthly, Quarterly and Yearly Meetings. These included Meetings for Worship, Meetings for Discipline, Meetings for Ministers and Elders, Meetings of Conference and Meetings for Worship to which the public were invited. The many occasions when *"I had a concern to hold a publick meeting"* were also fully recorded.

First Day and Weekday Meetings took place in Meeting Houses, where there was no Meeting House a room in a member's home was used. For Monthly, Quarterly and Yearly Meetings the accommodation varied greatly.

Those assembled in Meetings for Worship, on First days, or at times of Monthly, Quarterly and Yearly Meetings, believed that in the time they shared they could experience the divine presence. When uniting together, with their minds *"centered down deep in solemn silence",* it was possible to feel the presence and power of the Holy Spirit, *"under a feeling sense of his mercies in graciously condescending eminently to crown this Assembly with his divine presence"* (S.N.60 p10). It was then, *"in this state of pure silence in which the Lord's still small voice is heard and distinctly understood"* (L.N.17A p8), that an individual came to some understanding of *"the Lord's requirings"* of them and the word of God might be revealed in spoken ministry: *"It was a glorious Meeting, Truth had its testimony being exalted therein to the tendering of many minds* (S.N.16 p18) during which *"the various states of the people were in a very particular manner opened and spoke to, and the way of life and salvation clearly discovered and pointed out to the meanest capacity"* (S.N.60 p10).

When encouraging Charles Unsworth to *"faithfulness and diligence therein"* Joseph urged him as follows: *"when assembled endeavour to shut out all wanderings of the mind thus will thou be enabled to pray to thy Father which is in heaven in secret and he will reward thee openly, by lighting up the light of his glorious countenance upon thee, whereby thy heart will be broken and thy spirit contrited before him and thou enabled to worship him without the aid of words"* (L.N.33 p4).

On occasions he recorded being disheartened by the *"low, sluggish state"* of those attending, or thankful when the meeting was *"heavy and laborious in the forepart but ended comfortably"*. There were other times when he was joyfully uplifted, as when *"Truth arose in great dominion and caused the hearts of the patient waiters to rejoice"* or filled with renewed personal hope and optimism for the *"cause of truth"*.

Joseph always noted the names of those many Friends known as Strangers and Publick Friends, who, during their travels, were present at the Meetings he attended. (See Appendix 3) He valued both their company and their ministry. Commenting on the length of spoken ministry, those who gave testimony are described as having *"dropt a few words"*, or as having *"stood a long time"*, *"a pretty long time"* and *"a very long time"*. Biblical references were usually recorded, these having a particular significance for Joseph. When referring to the nature of what was spoken, he described a person as having been "favoured", "highly favoured" or as *"having been opened in an extraordinary manner"* or that *"living and powerful Testimonies were borne therein for our mutual comfort and edification"*. He was deeply concerned when inappropriate words were uttered, as at the Meeting when the son of Henry Swire was buried: *"it was a solemn weighty meeting but was hurt in the forepart by an unsanctified appearance"* (L.N.37 p18).

He also recorded those who were involved in supplication, exhortation, prayer and prayer and praises.

Meetings for Discipline had a particular significance for Joseph, for speaking as "he was led in a plain close manner to the unfaithful professors of truth", though he had "the word of consolation to the rightly exercised" (J. W.Testimony Pontefract Mo.Mg.). He was greatly concerned for those who appeared to him to be failing in their responsibilities of their profession and always sought to support them as their returned to live in *"the narrow way"*. However, *"if private labour prove ineffectual and they refuse to hear the Church"* his view, as expressed to Thomas Camm, was that *"it is necessary for Truth to be cleared by setting the offender without the camp for healing that so the Lord may be pleased to own our Assemblies with his presence, which will not be the case if true judgement is not placed upon the head of the transgressor"*. (L.N.33 p17). His insistence that the behaviour of members of the Meeting should be consistent with their profession was fully recognized: "that our dear friend was zealous for the proper support of discipline in our religious body was sufficiently evident from the part he took in the exercise of it in his own Monthly Meeting, for active service in this important branch of church government he was eminently gifted" (J.W. Testimony Pontefract Mo.Mg.).

It was at these Meetings that the Queries were read and answered from all the Monthly Meetings after which *"many weighty and instructive remarks were made thereon upon the deficiencies which appeared".*

Of the many other administrative and organisational issues that came before these Meetings, Joseph always noted how these were dealt with: *"Business was gone thro' in much Brotherly love and condescension"* or *"to pretty good satisfaction",* or *"amicably transacted to the solid satisfaction of the rightly exercised".* There were some occasions, however, when this had not been the case, as happened at a Winter Quarterly Meeting in Leeds: *"A great deal of business was gone thro' and tho' in the course thereof, some controversy appeared which brought pain over some exercised minds and hurt the solemnity of the meeting, yet at length truth prevailed and upon the whole I hope it was a profitable time, to the letting some active members see that tho' openings to service may be right, yet if it is supported in the will of the creature it will not tend to the honour and glory of great Name"* (L.N.24 p5) or when differing opinions were expressed in a Meeting for Discipline in Burton (Barnsley): *"The business of this meeting was in the general satisfactorily conducted, except one case in which there appeared to be diversity of sentiments which took up a considerable but at length was settled pretty well for the present"* (S.N.33 p15).

It is perhaps difficult to envisage the numbers attending major Quaker gatherings and the associated Meetings for Worship to which the general public were invited. Joseph's accounts provide an insight into the organisation needed to manage the numbers involved. These were so great that alternative or additional venues had to be found and frequently this needed to be done at the very last moment. At many of the Quaker Meetings which were *"not select of Friends"* Joseph described how those who *"came in"* to worship included *"People of other Societies"*, and local inhabitants. These were members of independent chapels, in particular the Methodists, and their Ministers and Class Leaders; those who attended the Parish Church and their Priest; members of the local gentry and many *"sober people"*. His experience in Nantwich was typical: *"the Meetinghouse was wellfill'd and the day being fair friends set open the sashes and the publick friends sat by them without doors, the Graveyard tho' large being likewise pretty near full of People"* (S.N.4 p29). At a public meeting held during the General Meeting for Derbyshire at Castleton in 1789 *"there was the largest number of people collect together that ever I saw at any General meeting, many computed there to be about 2000 and some thought considerably more"* (S.N.13 p16).

In Newtown, at the time of a Welsh Yearly Meeting, the first Meeting for Worship was held *"in the Market house under the Town hall which friends had fitted up for the occasion and got well seated and a convenient Gallery erected, one side being left open on purpose to accommodate the People for the house was quite crowded and the street also as far as they could hear with Persons of different persuasions and degrees".* After the Bellman gave notice on market day of a second public meeting and papers had been *"stuck up in the Town"* Joseph wrote that *"an abundance of more people from a great distance was come to Town this Afternoon far more than friends could hear at the Market house, so they concluded to divide and hold two meetings at one time, they easily got an empty Barn belonging to Sir John Price for the occasion and a very great crowd there was at both places"* (S.N.4 p2).

Joseph described occasions when it had been necessary to construct a Booth in which meetings would be held. These, it would appear, were a feature of many large gatherings. In Stockport, for instance, *"a large Booth built with boards on purpose for the occasion 31 yards long and 26 wide the erecting of which cost 80£"* (S.N.25 p6). At a Quarterly Meeting in Ulverston the public meeting for Worship *"was held in the Booth which was a place built of boards on purpose for the occasion and was large and well contrived being erected on a rising ground with the Gallery at the Bottom, so that people could see over one anothers heads, which was of great advantage to the meeting as at times many People attend who are not satisfied without they can see as well as hear"* (S.N.10 p21).

Those attending a Northern Yearly Meeting held in Rochdale met *"in a large Booth 30 yards long and 27 broad, having a Wood frame with scoured woollen pieces nailed thereto within and without and thatched with straw".* The second public Meeting for Worship *"was very much crowded and many could not get in so that friends divided"* and it was necessary to hold *"another meeting at the same time in a large Assembly room at the Flying Horse Inn".* For the third and final public meeting it was necessary to use the Booth, the Assembly room at the Flying Horse and an additional room in the Black Bull in order to accommodate the great *"concourse of people"* (S.N.14 p11).

The numbers attending a Northern Yearly Meeting in Nantwich were such that Joseph also noted: *"the Constables stood with their staffs in their hands at the booth doors to keep the people quiet if any should offer to make a disturbance and was very useful in helping to direct People to their seats"* (S.N.4 p29).

The holding of public meetings was of the utmost importance to Joseph and was a major and significant part of his ministry. Frequently he recorded: *"Having for some time past a concern upon my mind to have a Publick Meeting with the inhabitants of............."* (S.N.60 p14). It was also not unusual for him to have such a meeting when visiting a Meeting that was experiencing a decline in numbers or spontaneously as he was passing through a town or village on his travels.

The majority of Joseph's public meetings were, however, held in places where there were no Friends living. "His heart being enlarged in gospel love he was anxious for the salvation of all and was frequently engaged to appoint meetings amongst those not in profession with us. For this service he was eminently gifted and his ministry on these occasions was often attended with the powerful baptising influence of the spirit to the convincement of many" (J. W. Testimony Pontefract Mo.Mg.).

In a place *"that knew not of the principles of our profession"* Joseph would hire the Chapel of another protestant congregation in which to conduct the meeting, as when William Taylor of Barnsley wrote to him: "I was requested by John Yeardley, to indeavour to obtain leave, from the Methodists in Cudworth for thee to hold a publick meeting in have done so and have their consent" (J.W.Misc.Papers). If there was not a chapel or meetinghouse available then a public room, school room, a room in an inn or a barn might be hired or the use of rooms in the house of *"a sympathizing friend"* would be offered.   During many of his journeys Joseph held numerous such meetings. When sixty-eight years old on his return after a six week journey, he noted: *"I have further to remark that in the course of this visit I had 20 Publick Meetings in places were Meetings are not usually held and 8 of these no friends could remember any meetings of our Society being ever held in those places before"* (S.N.60 p8).

Such meetings were central to his service to the Lord, but, as with other aspects of his ministry, there were times of hesitancy and apprehension, as happened prior to a meeting in Emley *"I went in great Poverty of Spirit and under considerable discouragement of mind, there never having been a meeting of friends in Emley and the Inhabitants being entire strangers to me"* (S.N.21 p1).   It would appear however that Joseph relished the opportunities that public meetings provided for him to bring the gospel message to as many as felt *"the inclination to attend."*   The number of people in the congregation on these occasions could have been anywhere between a dozen to several hundred: *"12 friends attended", " I suppose there were about 300 Persons", "I think there were about 600 people friends and others".*

It was customary for Joseph as he closed a meeting to make a commendatory speech in which he thanked the People *"for their company"* and *"their attention and their good and solid behaviour".*   It was a rare occasion when this was not the case. At Matlock he expressed his sorrow as he acknowledged *"the hurt to the Meeting"* caused *"by those who arrived so much behind the appointed time"* (S.N.60 p3), or as happened in Belper *"the very unsettled behaviour of a few in keeping going in and out to their own hurt and the disturbance of others"* (S.N.60 p3) and in Barnsley when those attending *"appear'd light airy and Talkative* but *on being reprov'd by our Friend John Lupton were more moderate for sometime but afterwards fell too much into their old practice again".* (S.N.10 p5).

Joseph and his companions would frequently distribute books or pamphlets to those leaving a Publick Meeting. Writing his account of such a Meeting held in Wooldale he recorded: *"I put 20 small books into the hands of William Taylor to distribute to the People which he did at the Burial-ground-gate, they appearing to receive them with thankfulness"* (S.N.33 p5).

Meetings for Ministers and Elders held a specific place in Joseph's commitment to his ministry. The Elders of a Meeting were entrusted with the task of ensuring sound doctrine, but they also carried a major responsibility for the care and support of the Ministers within their Meeting and for the state of their spiritual well-being. Many Quakers in Joseph's time saw the authority of Ministers and Elders as essential to the maintaining of the *"ancient testimonies"* of Quaker Truth.

The importance these meetings had for Joseph is evident from his regular attendance. A significant part of the business for those so gathered at his own Monthly Meeting was to read and answer the Queries particular to these Meetings. Representatives were then appointed who would submit the Answers to the Meeting for Ministers and Elders held during the next Quarterly Meeting. Joseph faithfully recorded the names of those appointed to oversee the various Meetings held at such times and the fact that they reported to the Ministers and Elders how they had undertaken their responsibilities. For those who, like Joseph, laboured to further the cause of Quaker Truth the support and encouragement provided by these Meetings was greatly valued, for they usually closed after *"much weighty counsel and advice was dropt to us in these stations by sundry friends"* (L.N.24 p5)

To Friends within the Counties of Durham & Northumberland, & some parts of the North of Yorkshire.

Dear Friends

Our Esteemed Friend Joseph Wood, having spread before our last Monthly Meeting, the Women Friends also being present, a concern which had for a considerable time rested upon his mind to pay a religious visit to Friends in the Counties of Durham and Northumberland, also to some in the North parts of Yorkshire; as well as to have a few Meetings with Persons who are not of our Religious Persuasion in those parts; these are to certify concerning him, that he is a Minister approved by us; & we feeling Unity with him in his prospect and encouraged to hope, that his Labours may tend to the edification of those who are visited; and that he may on his Return experience the rich Reward of Peace.

Record of the unity of the members of Pontefract Monthly Meeting with Joseph's concern to visit Meetings in Durham, Northumberland and North Yorkshire in 1812

(S.N.50 p5)

Meeting Houses Joseph visited in North Yorkshire, and Northumberland in 1812

Guisborough Meeting House

Skipton Meeting House Ministers Stand

David Butler

Castleton
Meeting House
Interior

Allendale
Meeting House

Derwent Meeting House, Winnows Hill

David Butler

Letters

Copies of letters written by Joseph between 1797 and 1821 are contained in the Letter Books, 8, 10, 12, 14, 15, 17A, 19,21, 22, 26, 27 and 33.

Index to Large Notebook 21

Joseph thought of his correspondence as an essential part of his ministry. Reading his letters, one is aware of his overwhelming concern for the spiritual life of individuals and the destiny of their souls. His letters were the outcome of *"promptings"* received when in his *"secret retirement"* before the

Lord or as he was *"set musing in* [his] *chamber"*.

He wrote to people he saw frequently, whose homes he visited and with whom he had often had opportunities for conversation.   Clearly he considered the advantage of a letter was that it could be read and retained for future consideration.

Moreover, he was well aware that his correspondents might show his letters to others.   Indeed, he sometimes asked for this to be done. On certain occasions, however, for personal reasons, he requested that his letter be kept private. Likewise, those writing to him sometimes requested that he "keep this communication secret." Betty Booth, for example, wrote asking "I hope thou wont publish wat I rote in this paper for I shod not rote wat I have if I thought thou wood, but I think I durst trust the" (J.W. Misc. Papers).

When he was at home, it was his custom every morning after breakfast, to retire and spend time in quiet meditation, reading and writing. His letters frequently contained observations such as the following: *"I have felt a concern upon my mind on thy account"* or *"thou was suddenly and very unexpectedly brought before the view of my mind"* or *"Thou has been of late much the companion of my thoughts"*.   In a second letter he commented *"when I had wrote the forgoing I found my mind considerably relieved but since my exercise on thy account hath returned I shall not be easy without adding......."* (L.N.10 p4).

The majority of the letters were written in *"brotherly love"*, *"Christian love"* or in *"gospel love"* and were sent as from, *"thy well wishing friend"*, *"thy sincere friend"*, *"thy sympathizing friend"* or *"thy affectionate friend"*. In many of them Joseph expressed to the recipient his *"strongest desires for thy present and everlasting welfare"* or his concern for his or her *"welfare in time and eternity".*

There were occasions, too, when Joseph appears to have experienced a degree of doubt, hesitancy or even reluctance when faced with what he felt was asked of him. Writing to James Harrison, he admitted *"having been many times discouraged from the frequent low state of my own mind, and a fear of moving before my guide, and doing thee harm instead of good knowing that the Almighty is altogether sufficient for his own work"* (L.N.21 p5).

 Sometimes, sensing it was his duty to communicate his thoughts he would explain how he would not be *"clear in the sight of God"* unless he wrote to them. In such a manner, he reprimanded Sarah Bottomley who, in his view, had acted *"so inconsistently with Truth"* that he felt compelled to write to her: *"I have endeavoured to surpress the concern, yea, at times almost determined not to give up to it yet I find my peace so much concerned with my obedience that through many deep Baptisms unknown to any but the Lord alone I have been brought to a state of resignation to say Not my will but thine O Lord be done in me and by me. If thou will graciously condescend to go before me I will follow thee according to the best of my understanding"* (L.N.12 p7).

Joseph's thorough knowledge of both Old and New Testaments was apparent in his efforts to focus the attention of his readers and to verify the sacred Truth contained in what he had written: *"my earnest desire is that thou may not read it as a matter of little concern but solidly weigh the truths contained therein in a disposition of mind to improve thereby"* (L.N.10 p4).

The recipients of his letters also included some he knew could not read. In such cases, he expressed his hopes that there would be someone who could read the letters to them. To Joseph Grayham he wrote: *"Oftens have I felt a desire to attend my mind for thy eternal welfare but knew not which way most profitably to communicate it to thee, as I understand thou was under the disadvantage, that thou could neither read nor write, but the way I am upon felt most easy to me, hoping that some kind friend would take the trouble of reading it to you"* (L.N.15 p9) and to his great friend, Henry Swire of Totties *"the impression remaining upon my mind to write to thy Nephew I have herewith inclosed a Letter for him, which I request you will at some suitable opportunity when ye can be alone, and enjoy a time of stillness without outward interruption, thou'll be so kind as to read it to him; and that when it is done put it into his hands to preserve and read at his leisure"* (L.N.14 p9).

Many letters were written to express his approval of those desiring *"to seek after truth"* and to convey his support and encouragement to *"those coming forward in the service".* To those who were responding positively to some circumstance relating to their faith there were letters nourishing and strengthening their resolve. To the newly convinced Friends in Barnsley he wrote: *"For Jonathan Bashforth, Thomas Walton, Thomas Walker Haigh, James Wood, Isabella Bashforth, Elizabeth Dunn, Elizabeth Wilson, and Ellen Spenceley*

I have felt my mind drawn under the pure influence of Gospel love to write to you; and though I am sensible, that your states are widely different, yet I believe all of you have been overshadowed with that heavenly Power, Light and Life, which comes by Jesus Christ: and which, if you are concerned to seek often no other knowledge but what comes from his divine principle placed in the secret of each heart; and are fully obedient to its discoveries, we lead all of you to a settlement upon that foundation which cannot be shaken. I have earnestly desired that one and all of you, may centre to down deep in your minds; and labour up after that state of pure silence, in which the Lords still small voice, is heard and distinctly understood.......". (L.N.17A p6).

A recurring theme was his insistence on attendance at First Day and Week Day Meetings. He warmly commended those who attended regularly, urged those who were no more than occasional attenders to consider the error of their ways and severely held to account those he considered guilty of neglecting this religious duty. He did, however, accept and understand the difficulties experienced by those suffering from genuine ill health.   He wrote reassuringly to his cousin Charles Stead junior: *"I doubt not but thou hast oftens lamented thy neglect of duty herein since the Lord hath been mercifully pleased to visit thee with his day spring from on high, yet he is no hard master, he is not requiring impossibilities of us, remembering his gracious promise I will have mercy not sacrifice. When those through affliction are deprived of the privilege of attending religious meetings he is pleased to enable them to worship alone in his presence"* (L.N.33 p8).

It was Joseph's conviction that all family living was to be arranged and business affairs managed so as to make attendance at Meetings possible.   Explaining this point to William Stead, he wrote: *"I have arose early when young in years to get forward with my business in order that I might not neglect this duty, and have gone out of the harvest field many times and washed me by the way at a spring"* (L.N.14 p3). To George Chapman he declared: *"there is one thing appears to me as a duty to offer to thy serious consideration, and that is the shutting up thy shop, during the time of Meeting on weekdays this at first may appear a tryal of faith, but if solidly weighed and found to be a duty, reason not with flesh and Blood, but give up faithfully, and the promise of Christ will be fulfilled to the, an hundredfold in this life and in that which is to come everlasting"* (L.N.8 p9).

Having no children of his own, Joseph took a great interest in the lives of his nephews and nieces and the families of friends. Giving his approval to his nephew, Robert Wood, for what he saw as an improvement in his dress and behaviour, Joseph wrote him a lengthy letter as his *"affectionate uncle",* commending his *"diligence in attending Meetings for Worship and discipline for some considerable time past and* [his] *behaviour therein and of late laying aside superfluities in* [his] *apparel and coming nearer that Plainness which Truths leads its faithful followers into; I would willingly hope is the product of the great husbandman in thy heart and must be satisfactory to faithful friends to observe who have no greater joy* than to see the youth desirous to walk in the Truth" (L.N.15 p13).

With a like concern for his much-loved cousin, Benjamin Stead, being conscious of failings in his religious duty, he wrote: *"my mind hath oftens been sorely affected by hearing of thee giving way to the unnecessary frequenting of Alehouses and drinking to excess When thou may be beset the temptations of this sort, consider how much drunkenness debases a man below the brute creation and what a sorrowful mispending of time it is, which is spent unnecessarily in Alehouses, which when it is over cannot be recalled. How much it unfits a man for religious duties, what a bad example it is to all the youths in their own families, and how it lessens their authority therein, for how can any degree of weight, advice or restrain the youth under their care for running into evil but, when they themselves are guilty of this heinous sin, and what is worst of all it not only destroys a man's health and reputation, but his poor never dying immortal soul, as we have it left upon record amongst many other evils which are enumerated, that no drunkard shall inherit the kingdom of God. Dear Cousin bear with patience my plain dealing. It is out of real respect, and from an apprehension of duty I thus write. I love thee and therefore am desirous thou should be preserved out of every thing that is a hurt to thy body or soul"* (L.N.12 p2).

The sin of drinking to excess troubled Joseph greatly, and many of his letters reflected this, even when one of those he felt compelled to write to was Elihu Dickinson, the Tanner, an Elder of his own Meeting. Writing *"in all the tenderness of a Brother and fellow member of the same Religious Society"* he urged him *"to guard against being inadvertently drawn to take more liquor than is really useful"* (L.N.12 p14).

Mindful of human folly and weakness Joseph expressed understanding of this condition but was forthright in his condemnation of sinful deeds. To those guilty of such actions he asserted *"bring reproach upon the Society of which you are a member and a great grief and exercise upon all the minds of those who wish thee well"* (L.N.12 p14). He encouraged many of those to whom he wrote: *"to renounce the follies and flesh pleasing vanities of this world that lieth in wickedness"* and *"to seek after the durable riches of eternity"* (L.N.26 p3).

Joseph never shrank from that which he believed was required of him in maintaining the discipline of those who erred from the *"strait way"*. To these people he wrote entreating them to greater watchfulness and to repentance, so, to Joseph Haigh junr. he wrote: *"I rejoiced exceedingly when I heard that thou was made sensible of thy late misconduct"* and later *"we may be ready to think we will never do the like again, yet if we are not concerned to keep a daily watch, and seek unto the Lord for strength we shall not be able to stand when he (the Devil) may be suffered to assult us"* (L.N.12 p14).

He cautioned those so admonished to refrain from the offending actions and urged them to repentance as he did Charles Smith: *"how great are his mercies to those who have deeply revolted and backsliden, when they are thus in an humble penitent state of mind, returning unto him, acknowledging their error, repenting, and doing their first works"* (L.N.14 p13).

For an unstated reason, he wrote to Joshua Roberts that he felt: *"a duty to communicate to thee after this manner with desires that thou may receive it in the Love in which it is wrote and that they may consider from whence thou art fallen and repent and do thy first works, lest the Lord should come unto thee quickly and remove thy candlestick out of its place. But alas how is it with thee now, how have thou turned back again to drink up of those rivers from which thou was once redeemed, and what is the cause; because thou refuse to attend to the language of the spirit and reject the advice of thy best friends, who saw the danger thou was in and was concerned to labour honestly and faithfully with thee. O suffer me to entreat thee in that pure love which dare not flatter or deceive, to return unto Bethel, to remember the time of thy tryed espousals and the covenants thou hast made in the days of thy youth; that so thou may sensibly perceive his call renewed unto thee and a disposition of mind to obey "O Israel return unto thy God for thou hast fallen by thine iniquity" then would thou witness his promise fulfilled "I will heal their backsliding, I will love them freely; for mine anger is turned away from him". Then my friend there would be a bringing forth fruit consistent with the principle we profess; and instead of being a stumbling block in the way of others, thou would be a light in the world and that this may be the case is what I much desire and travail in spirit for"* (L.N.8 p6).

Joseph wrote to those being asked to undertake a leading role in the work and organisation of the Meeting in order to dispel any fears or misgivings they might have had about their preparedness or ability to fulfil such responsibilities.

Joshua Earnshaw, a prominent member of the small Lumbroyd Meeting, received his support. Joseph, aware of the difficulties being faced by *"the very low and desolate state of your meeting"* advised him *"therefore be not too discouraged or cast down, but what thine hand findeth to do, do it with all thy might. This I believe is the way for a revival and to be favoured with true Peace"* (L.N.33 p8).

Having served on the committee charged with considering *"the names of suitable friends for Overseers"* he wrote to John Pickford: *"when thy name was proposed by a worthy friend and seconded by the feelings of another, the witness in me said Amen thereunto, and when the meeting confirmed the Proposition, I thought it was like the laying on of the hands of the Apostles, if thou on thy part was but sufficiently resigned, just to be and to do what the supreme head of the church saw meet for thee"* (L.N.14 p6).

On hearing that George Broadhead was being asked to accept the responsibilities of an Elder, Joseph, wishing to show his support for this proposal, wrote to him: *"therefore thou be encouraged to come forward in thy religious services, in the Name which is the Power of the Lord of Hosts; and I firmly believe that thou will be blessed to the good of others and thine own solid peace. Its needful that those who labour with other should keep their own garments unspotted of the world and tho' they may at times be dip'd* into a sense of their own weakness and see themselves unfit for the work; yet if watchful, will experience preservation. Thus may thou be made instrumental to turn many from the evil of their ways to righteousness; and to shine as a star in the firmament for ever" (L.N.8 p14).

Sometimes Joseph was called upon to act as a mediator between those who were parties to a disagreement or when difficulties arose. One such occasion was detailed in a letter written to Mary Johnson of Pontefract: "thou hast met with some discouragement from some friends of the Quarterly Meeting which hath made thee desirous to resign thy office of Clerk to the Monthly meeting. Now my friend I would tenderly advise thee to keep in meekness of true wisdom and closely guard every avenue where there maybe any danger of prejudice entering but at the same time desert not the cause. I understand thou hast offered to resign thy station or office. So far I believe thou has acted right but as the Womens Monthly Meeting are of the judgment that it is right for thee to continue; I believe it will be right and profitable for thee to submit thereto, and would advise thee to have thy will so much reduced into the innocency and simplicity of a little child as to be able to say the next opportunity thou art favoured with; That notwithstanding thou art free to decline the office thou art also free to continue it until friends find one that they apprehend will suit the place. Thus I believe thou will be favoured with peace in thy own mind and experience all things work for good" (L.N.14 p11).

A strong advocate of "the upholding of our Testimony against the payment of the Church Tythe, Rate or the Modus", Joseph staunchly refused to pay this tax. He constantly reminded others to do the same, urging them not to yield under the pressure from the Church authorities to do so. Neither were they to allow another person to pay the tax for them. In letters sent to Thomas West (L.N.14 p2) and John Allott (L.N.10 p16), he gave a full explanation why he and those like him resisted payment.

In like manner he appealed to those called to the militia to remain resolute in their refusal to serve and not to pay for another to take their place. In 1797, for instance, he wrote to Enoch Dickinson commending him for his courage in refusing to be balloted for the militia and encouraging him in his resolve, even in the light of certain punishment: *"Ever since I heard of thee being Ballotted to serve in the Militia, I have felt a secret sympathy with thee, accompanied with a hope that thou would be enabled to stand thy ground faithfully, in this day of trial, which I believe will try the foundations of many. It hath several times appeared to me as a duty to encourage thee to trust in the Lord with all thine heart, and then thou will not fear what man can do to thee, for his power only reaches over the body. Therefore my dear friend be encouraged to stand thy ground faithfully and if a Prison be thy lot, suffer cheerfully, thou'll have the tender sympathy of the spiritually minded and the reward of Peace in thy own bosom, the Prison walls will not be able to separate thee from it, and all things will work together for thy good"* (L.N.10 p12).

In his concern for those contemplating a change in the circumstances of their lives Joseph would often write urging them *"to seek the counsel of the Lord"* and that *"of faithful friends"* before making any decisions.

Strongly believing that marriage should only be with *"a member of our Society"* Joseph repeatedly gave advice to the young people of his acquaintance, as he did in the case of John Wood Broadhead: *"If thou should incline to enter into a married state be thou sure to chuse a sober young Woman and a member of the Society. Let me intreat thee therefore in this great and weighty undertaking if thou engaged therein, to seek the counsel of the Lord, and act faithfully to the good order established amongst us, and then I doubt not thou will be favoured with a true helpmeet"* (L.N.12 p10).

For the same reason he was prompted to write to those contemplating marriage with *"one of another persuasion",* as when he later wrote once more to John Wood Broadhead with this warning: *"for O the sorrowful work that mixt marriage hath made amongst us and with the offspring of such"* (L.N.12 p9). He would also write to the parents whose children had married out, as he did to Joseph Stead: *"believing that you discharged your duty by endeavour what lay in your power to prevent it, but I have sometimes thought whether there has not been more familiarity with them since than has been prudent"* (L.N.10 p6).

With a similar concern he felt compelled to write to those considering a marriage with next of kin. To Martha Haigh he had this to say: *"The peace of my own mind, which hath been many times heavily oppressed on thy account since I heard of thee letting out thy mind in relation to Marriage unto one so near of kin, looking upon it to be a deep laid snare of the enemy, if possible to frustrate the many divine visitations which I believe thou has been favoured with. Now I much desire for thine own sake and the sake of others who may be looking towards thee for example, that thou may seek unto the Lord for strength to overcome the present temptation for such connections appear to me not only unnatural but I believe quite contrary to the mind of Truth and are frequently attended with sorrow, disappointment and woe the portion of those who reject the reproofs of instruction and the tender advice of their best friends"* (L.N.14 p16).

To those planning to move house or seeking different employment Joseph warned of the dangers of such an undertaking. His counsel to Joseph Stead was this: *"Having several times heard that thou was unsettled in thy mind removing from thy present residence, I have desired that thou might seriously weigh the matter before thou take any steps in an affair of such importance. If thine dissatisfaction arises from outward courses, if thou should remove with a view to leave sorrow and trouble, thou will most assuredly find it in one kind or another where ever thou goest. For the Scripture declare "Man is born to trouble as the sparks fly upward" But many things are permitted to overtake us, in order*

98

to wean our minds from the breast of the world, but if when tryals overtake, and we suffer wrong and are afflicted, we become unsettled thereby and disturbed in our minds and think to get quit of these things by removing, depend upon it we shall find our sorrows instead of being mitigated thereby increase. It hath always appeared to me a matter of great importance to remove from place to another and indeed there is abundant cause to seek unto him for counsel, direction and instruction in such weighty concerns. Things at present outwardly wear a very gloomy appearance, but wither shall we flee to leave them, is it not the hand of the Lord in them, who fills both heaven and earth" (L.N.14 p16).

To Mark Breaer, who had *"given way to too much unprofitable conversation about removing to America"* Joseph expressed his deep concern about the proposed move *"much more so to such a distance as America"* and cautioned him that it had been *"observed that the dissolving of old and forming of new connections, have in many instances been attended with effect so prejudicial to a growth in the Truth; especially where the inclination to such removal hath originated in worldly motives"* (L.N.33 p17).

Anxious to alert John Brook to what might occur if he persisted with the decision to change his job, Joseph cautioned him: *"the enemy seeks to disturb, by making mankind believe they can be in some other place than where they are"* adding *"it is dangerous leaving a certainty for uncertainty, you may have promise of employment, but consider if your employer should be removed by death, perhaps a total disappointment may be the consequence, and ye thereby brought into very unforeseen straits and difficulties"* (L.N.15 p5).

To a cousin who had decided to move house and employment, he described how my *"mind hath oftens been affected with sorrow that so many of the members of our Society who are comfortably situated in the country, where they are favoured with every thing which nature requires, should leave these peaceful quiet habitations, and flock into Cities and great Towns and have oftens yea very oftens seen the sorrowful consequence thereof, for however they may have advanced themselves in the world thereby, very few according to my observation have advanced much in piety and virtue; Wherefore I cannot but much unite with many faithful friends in the beginning who bore their testimony against it, and had to see even in their day the sorrowful consequence of it, For by entering into large concerns in trade many got so leavened into the spirit of this World as almost wholly to depart from the plainness and simplicity of the pure Truth...."* (S.N.32 p13).

Joseph was very conscious of his responsibility to support and help maintain the faith of those experiencing difficulties and hardship in their lives. In kindly, gentle words he expressed his sympathy and compassion for them in their situation, "offering a word of consolation to the rightly exercised unto whom he was a nursing Father" (J.W. Testimony Pontefract Mo.Mg.).

The cause of the distress was seldom referred to, but he clearly stated the response that it should draw forth from those involved. Acknowledging the hand of Providence in all things, Joseph's advice was that they must not sink into *"murmuring and grumbling"* but to *"suffer all things with patience"* and look to the Lord for the help that only *"he can give in times of trouble".*

Quoting passages of Scripture as a way of illustrating his counsel and highlighting those from which comfort could be taken, he attempted to offer encouragement, as he did to Elihu Dickinson, whose wife was deeply disturbed: *"perhaps in mercy dispensed to us by the universal Parent of mankind, in order that we may not place our happiness in anything here below, but everything being thereby stained in our view we are wisely preparing for an inheritance incorruptible were all sorrows and tears will be wiped away. Those who are thus exercised will at all times be favoured in their passing along through this vale of tears with a foretaste of the joys that are to come, which sweetens the many bitter cups we may have to drink, and the deep trials we may have to pass through. Thine my friend oftens appear to me to be of the nearest and deepest kind, and may I truly say my spirit according to my measure nearly sympathises with thee, and am frequently led secretly to breathe(pray) that thou may be supported under them, so as not to sink too low in spirits or injure thy health, and I believe as a Man and a Christian it is thy duty to endeavour to bear thy heavy afflictions as patiently as thou can, and then no doubt divine support will be near to bear up thy poor drooping mind, and thou wilt experience though painful days and wearisome nights may be allotted thee, yet all things will work together for good"* (L.N.14 p4).

Joseph was sensitive to the pain and anguish parents suffered at the death of a child and wrote with tenderness and much understanding of the profound sorrow felt by the bereaved at such a time, urging them to seek from the Lord the strength to say *"not my will but thy will".* Writing to John and Ann Firth, he expressed his *"tender sympathy with you this present occasion I believe it is a near thing for parents to bury a child but there is this consolation; that it is taken from the troubles of the time into a happy Eternity. David on a similar occasion says Sam. C. 12. v. 23. Now he is dead wherefore should I fast? Can I bring him back again? I shall go to him but he shall not return to me. Now Dear friends consider this seriously and I believe that tho' nature must have a little vent, it will moderate your grief"* (L.N.8 p5).

Since the hand of God was to be found in all things, when both parents of John Wood Broadhead died, Joseph wrote to him offering sympathy and support but only after urging him in a most direct, even harsh, manner to reflect on some unspecified aspects of his behaviour and the Lord's dealings with such as him: *"I cannot but sympathize with thee under a sense of the loss thou has sustained in the removal of thy Parents whose counsel and advice in the ordering of best wisdom my desire is that thou may be favoured to seek after and attain to a state of true resignation; and then it may prove a blessing to thee, as the most high hath many ways of bringing poor man to the knowledge of himself sometimes he allures the mind,* and draws it as by the cords of divine love, but when he works the enemy works also and too often prevails to settle the mind in a state of ease and indifferency again, and so puts off the day of visitation to some future period, altho' we are sensible our time is not our own, nor knows not that we may be favoured to see another day. Yet such is the regard of the most high that he continues graciously to call unto those who have rejected the offers of his love, and visits them by his judgements mixed with mercy, sometimes casting them upon a sick bed, and sometimes removing their near and dear connections from them in order that they may see the uncertainty of time, and seek after a right preparation for an endless eternity. And when I have considered the many removals in so short a space of time in your family I have earnestly desired, that it may be a means of turning thy feet into that path which will most assuredly terminate in Peace" (L.N.12 p9).

Joseph was greatly distressed and suffered *"deep exercise of spirit"* at the sickness and death of Robert Grayham, aged three years, the only son of his *"beloved scholar Joseph Grayham"*. Robert had been a regular and much-welcomed visitor at Newhouse, brought by his father to the man who had played such an important role in his life, Joseph having been his teacher, his employer and his dependable friend in difficult times. Describing his relationship with the child, Joseph wrote: *"I was remarkable fond of and he of me I found him much worse than I expected taking but little notice of anything I was speaking to him he put his little hands as usual for me to take him, he sat up on my knee but took little notice. I was much affected to see him so poorly and so loving",* and after his death *"I think I cannot but add that he was a child I loved more than any I knew for tho' he was a naturally of a reserved disposition, yet he always manifested such a particular attachment to me from the time of his being capable of notice, as never any other did, so that it exceedingly endeared him to me, and after he got as he could talk his expressions of love and regard for me, were oftens affecting to my mind and I believe will never be erased whilst I am favoured with memory"* (L.N. 30 p18).

The following *"Lines on Robert Graham a favourite child"* composed at the time demonstrate his deep feelings at this sad event

> *"My Robert has left me, and he is gone;*
> *His outward absence, now I do bemoan.*
> *He was a child, to me lovely and dear;*
> *I greatly did desire, his presence here;*
> *His sincere love, endeared him much to me.*
> *He certainly was a fine, and witty Boy;*
> *His Fathers darling, and his Mothers joy.*
> *Beloved by me, as my adopted child;*
> *Who in his sickness, neither wept nor smild.*
> *Who bore it throughout, with becoming mie;*
> *Tho' great his pain, he mostly kept serene.*
> *His looks at me, when near unto his end;*
> *Conveyed last love, of a departing Friend.*
> *Ah! now he's gone, his maker saw it best;*
> *Early to take him, to eternal rest.*
> *For he who gave him life, took it again;*
> *I mourn my loss, yet dare not I complain.*
> *But beg to be resigned, to Gods will;*
> *For he is worthy, to be served still."*   (L.N.30 p19)

Selected Quaker Writings

Many of Joseph's Notebooks contain articles, epistles, letters, memoirs, testimonials and poems which, it would seem, had a particular significance for him. Worthy of being retained, either because of the nature of the content or his knowledge of the writer, these were copied into both the Small Notebooks 2,6,7,8,9, and Large Notebooks 1-7,9,11,13,16-18,20,23,25,29-32,34-37. The body of literature circulating amongst Meetings and between individuals was of immense importance to Friends and was welcomed by them as a means of enriching their religious life and deepening their understanding of their faith.

Papers relating to the life and organisation of the Society of Friends were in plentiful supply and were available to all members through their Meetings. The Epistles written after major Meetings, in which Advice and Queries were set down and were regularly circulated, as were the letters written by those who had undertaken Visitations. These contained comments on the state of the Meetings and the attending families and also the recommendations and advice that had been given. There were also documents produced both by the Yearly Meeting and by individuals to highlight national and international issues of interest to Quakers.

Of equal importance were epistles, essays and letters written by individuals. A prime concern of those entrusted with the duty of furthering spiritual truth was the personal responsibility to record their faith, convincement and the Lord's dealings with them. These accounts were then made available to others so that they may benefit from reading about such experiences. These were written with the intention of being made public whilst others were sent as private correspondence but with the understanding that the recipient may let others read them.

104

Index to Large Notebook 1

Articles relating to matters of concern from a newspaper or acceptable magazine were also circulated. Papers were made available to Joseph by the Friends he knew in the various Meetings he attended and many have survived and give an insight into the amount of copying of documents that was undertaken and the extent of the reciprocal arrangements for their distribution. Joseph King, with whom Joseph had a lifelong correspondence, wrote to him in 1775: "I think it quite right where there is proper freedom for friends to assist each other in procuring of this kind of Papers" and in 1776 "when it suits thy Convenience please send me a List of thy valuable Manuscripts and I shall in return forward thee a List of mine, by wch we will be better able to Judge what is most Proper and suitable to forward each other Copies of in the future." and again in 1787 "if thou have got any new Manuscript Lately wch can communicate shall be obliged with Perusing one or two of thine having got none myself lately" (J.W. Misc. Papers).

Joseph was also fortunate in that, when travelling and visiting Friends, he had the opportunity to browse the contents of his host's library or collection of writings. When attending the Spring Quarterly Meeting in Leeds in 1800 of his visit to David Jepson he noted: *"I tarried a considerable time he shewing me a collection of Letters of many of our ancient friends in their own handwriting which he had collected and preserved very entire by sewing them together, and were directed to different persons, being from George Fox, James Naylor, William Dewsbury, Richard Farnsworth, Alexander Parker, Christopher Taylor, Thomas Aldham, Gervas Benson, Margaret Fell, and many others"* (S.N.33 p3). On the occasions when he saw papers that were of interest to him it is clear that he was able to request copies.

Joseph's belief in the all-pervading hand of Providence is reflected in the inclusion in his Notebooks of the reports of others recounting the Lord's dealings with them. It is also revealed in several accounts of unusual and inexplicable events or situations.

For many Friends the reality and influence of the Lord were to be found in dreams and visions. These were understood to be a way in which the Lord entered human thought and understanding. Frequently, if responded to, they helped an individual to take a particular course of action or behave in a certain way. Joseph accepted these mystical experiences and included accounts of several recalled by others, one of which directly concerned him (L.N.23 p3).

Many of the writings selected by Joseph reflected his keen awareness of mortality and contained constant warnings that people should *"be ever prepared for their final change"*.

Religious poems were a very acceptable form in which to express spiritual beliefs and Joseph copied a number into his Notebooks.

There are numerous accounts of the travels and experiences in foreign countries written by those who, in order to fulfil their religious ministries, journeyed to America, the West Indies, France, the Channel Isles and Ireland.   In addition to the religious content inherent in such writings, the descriptions they contained of faraway places, of their inhabitants and of events that occurred provided the reader with exciting adventure stories.

Pamphlets

1. A Sermon delivered at Leeds by S: Fothergill
2. Reasons for quitting the Methodists Society by John Helton.
3. Select pieces on religious subjects by Isaac Pennington.
4. Reasons for the necessity of Silent waiting in order for the solemn worship of God by Mary Brook
5. Deborah Bells Journal.
6. The deplorable State of Man & his redemption by Jesus Christ extracted from a late author by John Helton.
7. The fighting sailor turnd peaceable Christian.
8. Some expressions of Anne Cowley during her last illness.
9. An Epistle to Friends in Great Britain or elsewhere by David Hall.
10. An address to the inhabitants of Pennsylvania
11. Poems by John Fry.
12. Considerations touching the likeliest means to remove hirelings out of the Church by Jn°. Milton
13. 2 Sermons Preached at York by Thomas Story.
14. Remarks on an address to the People called Quakers by S: Fothergill.
15. A serious address to such as are concerned in commerce & Trading by Ambrose Rigge.
16. Method of managing Bees.

A page from Notebook II in which Joseph listed his books and pamphlets in 1778

A PERSONAL CONCLUSION

It is fortunate that a portrait of Joseph has survived so that we know what he looked like. From this it is not difficult to imagine his bearing and his physical presence.

Whilst transcribing the Notebooks, I have found myself drawn into Joseph's world, his experiences and the manner of his life. I have shared in the pleasures, the sorrows, the satisfactions and the disappointments. I am well acquainted with his regular habits and the routines of his daily living. I am fully aware of his well organised, methodical and pragmatic approach to all his undertakings.

Having come to recognise the great love that he had for his fellow human beings I am sure that it was his unpretentious, forthright manner coupled with a compassionate nature that endeared him to so many of those who knew him. The kindly assistance he received when he was experiencing ill health, and as he grew older, was given by people who clearly went out of their way to help him. I am certain this was an expression of their regard and fondness for him.

The overwhelming impression I have of Joseph is that in this man every part of his being, all his actions and his endeavours were realised totally within the context of his unshakable faith. Founded on the ancient simplicity of the Truth as spoken by the prophets and the forefathers, this was one of spiritual hope and aspiration.

Joseph Wood was indeed "the quintessence of a Quaker of the Quietist age" (Bower and Knight).

APPENDICES

Appendix 1   Sources

Manuscripts

Wood, Joseph: Collection of Miscellaneous Papers.

Wood, John: An Account of the Wood family   1880

Records of Pontefract Monthly Meeting

Printed Books

Bower, David. Knight, John: Plain Country Friends The Quakers of Wooldale, High Flatts and Midhope, Wooldale Meeting of Society of Friends   1987

Braithwaite, Joseph: (ed), Memoirs of Joseph John Gurney Fletcher and Alexander   1854

Butler, David M: Quaker Meeting Houses of Great Britain Vol.1 and Vol.2 Quaker Historical Society   1999

Dandelion, Ben Pink: Quaker Quietism: distinct or definitive Quaker Quarterly Issue One,   2010

Evans, W. and Evans, T.: (ed), Memoirs of Thomas Scattergood Gilpin   1845

Frost, J.   Recollections of James Jenkins   Mellen Press   1984

Loukes, Harold: The Quaker Contribution   SCM Press Ltd,   1965

Mills, John Travis: John Bright and the Quakers   Methuen, 1935

Parry, Owen: Welsh Quakers in the light of the Joseph Wood Papers The Celtic Bulletin Vol.24,   1972-1974

Scott, Samuel: A Diary of some religious exercises and experience Philadelphia, U.S.A.,   1811

Shillitoe, Thomas: Journal of the Life, Labours and Travels of John Shillitoe Harvey and Darton,   1839

Thistlethwaite, W. Pearson: Yorkshire Quarterly Meeting 1665-1966 Harrogate 1979

Tylor, Charles: (ed), Memoir and Diary of J. Yeardley Minister of the Gospel, London 1859

Tylor, Charles: Samuel Tuke; His life, work and thoughts, Headley Bros. 1900

Wood, Joseph: Large and Small Notebooks   2010   See Appendix 2

Other

Samuel, Bill: Quietists in the 18th. Century   www.quakerinfo.com

Appendix 2   Libraries and Archives

The original Large and Small Notebooks of Joseph Wood and the Collection of Miscellaneous Papers are to be deposited in the Archives at Friends House, Euston Road, London.

It is envisaged that a copy of the full transcript of the Large and Small Notebooks of Joseph Wood will be available from early 2011 in the following Libraries and Archives:

> The Library and Archives, Friends House, London
> Woodbrooke Quaker Study Centre, Birmingham
> The Brotherton Library, University of Leeds
> The Religious Studies Library, University of Lancaster
> The Archives, University of Huddersfield
> Hull History Centre, Hull
> The Local Studies Library, Public Library, Huddersfield
> West Yorkshire Archive Service, Wakefield
> Aberystwyth University, Aberystwyth, Wales

> Ireland Library, Quaker House, Dublin, Ireland

> Earlham College, Richmond, Indiana, U.S.A.
> Guilford College, Greensboro, South Carolina, U.S.A.
> Haverford College, haverford, Pennsylvania, U.S.A.
> Pendle Hill College, Wallingford, Pennsylvania, U.S.A.
> Swarthmore College, Swarthmore, Pennsylvania, U.S.A.

Appendix 3

Pamela Cooksey - publications planned for 2011

> Quaker Families noted in the writings of Joseph Wood (1750-1821) A Yorkshire Quaker
> Strangers and Publick Friends noted in the writings of Joseph Wood (1750-1821) A Yorkshire Quaker

Appendix 4

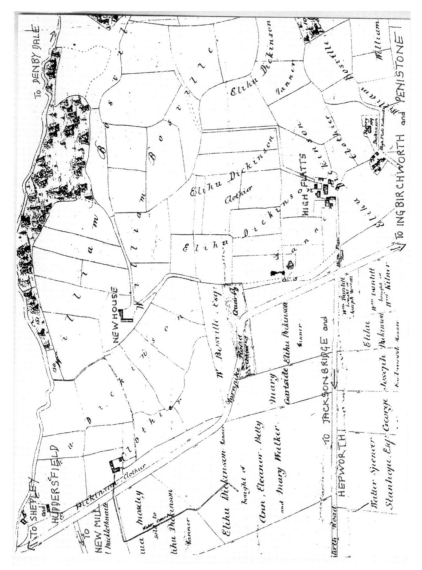

Sketch map based on the Denby and Clayton West Inclosure Award
Map 1804 showing High Flatts and Newhouse

(courtesy of W.Y.A.S. Kirklees. Ref: Den/SR2)

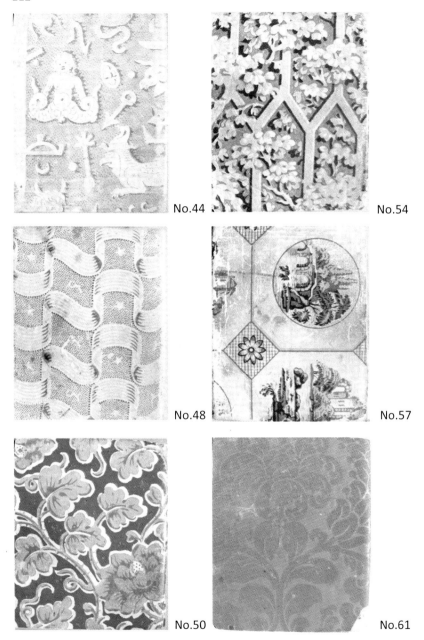

No.44

No.54

No.48

No.57

No.50

No.61

Examples of the covers of the Small Notebooks